THE PERSON OF CHRIST

Volume I: The Doctrine

In preparation by the same Author

THE PERSON OF CHRIST

Volume II: The Logos and Messiah
Volume III: The Lord and Servant
Volume IV: The King and Son of Man

THE PERSON OF CHRIST

Volume I: THE DOCTRINE

H. BRASH BONSALL, M.A., B.D.
Principal of The Birmingham Bible Institute

With Foreword by

F. F. BRUCE, M.A., D.D.
Rylands Professor of Biblical Criticism and Exegesis in the University of Manchester

CHRISTIAN LITERATURE CRUSADE
LONDON

CHRISTIAN LITERATURE CRUSADE
51 The Dean, Alresford, Hants, SO24 9BJ

U.S.A.
Fort Washington, Pa.

AUSTRALIA
Pennant Hills, N.S.W.

NEW ZEALAND
Box 1688, Auckland, C.1

also in

Europe, Canada
Central America, South America,
West Indies, Africa, India,
Indonesia, Far East

Reprinted 1982

*Printed in Great Britain by Richard Clay (The Chaucer Press) Ltd,
Bungay, Suffolk*

FOREWORD

THE relation between the Jesus of History and the Christ of Faith is a subject of prime importance, however it is regarded, and one that has been variously assessed at different times. Two generations ago it was widely believed that the Christ of Faith must go, but that the Jesus of History was both ascertainable and acceptable. Further study of the Gospels made this position untenable. Form criticism of the Gospels made it plain that even the earliest Synoptic strata, which had been relied upon as a basis for the reconstruction of the "historical" Jesus, emphasize the theological significance of all that Jesus did and said. "We can find no alternative tradition," wrote Professor C. H. Dodd, "excavate as we will in the successive strata of the gospels" (*History and the Gospel*, 1938, p. 103). But while Professor Dodd's conclusion was that the theological or messianic portrayal of Jesus had therefore strong claims to be accepted as the authentic and historical portrayal, it is commonly said today that since the Gospel material is theological through and through, the history eludes us almost completely. We are advised to come to terms with this state of affairs and be thankful for the theology, since we cannot have the history; indeed, we are told that to hanker after the Jesus of History betrays a lack of faith and an unworthy craving to know "Christ after the flesh".

What I like most of all about this study by Principal Brash Bonsall is his insistence that the Jesus of History and the Christ of Faith cannot be separated, that they are one and the same Jesus Christ, that the history and the theology are inextricably interwoven. St. John knew what he was about when he emphasized that the Logos became flesh, that "Jesus of Nazareth, the son of Joseph", as His contemporaries called Him, was not only the one "of whom Moses in the law, and also the prophets, wrote", but the perfect revelation in time of the eternal God. Because this identity of the historical Jesus with the Christ of experience and confession is so clearly brought out here, I hope that these studies, prepared in the first instance for the students of The Birmingham Bible Institute, will be made available to a wider public, to whom I am happy to commend them.

F. F. BRUCE

To my wife

PREFACE

THE present study has been designed to help the Christian reader with limited experience in theology to grasp some of the elementary Bible principles about the Person of Christ. This volume covers in a basic way the greater part of the subject and is complete in itself. It aims to provide a sort of primary glossary of theological concepts needed for advanced study.

Three further volumes are being prepared, to complete the Series. Volume Two will present Christ as the Word (*Logos*) and the Messiah, and attention will be centred upon the Gospels. Volume Three will show Him as Lord (*Kurios*) and attention will be focused on Acts, on its Proclamations (*Kerygmata*) and on the Life of the Early Church. The challenge of Rudolph Bultmann will be faced at this juncture. Volume Four will reveal Christ as the future King and Final Deliverer and treat those Scriptures relating to the Second Coming.

The Four Volumes will between them cover the main aspects of the Doctrine of the Person of Christ.

Instruction has been combined with Bible Study to help the Reader see how the Scriptures give their own answers to every question put by Theology. It is designed to aid him to go to the Book itself with every problem and to trace every doctrine down to the soil whence it sprang.

No necessary technical term is bypassed, and each new one is explained directly it is used. By the "Spiral Method", the doctrines are first presented as a general panorama and then the same ground is gone over again and they are shown in detail. This is the natural way both to teach and to learn and the repetition involved is designed to keep vital truths fixed in the mind.

An informal style has been adopted, and stories and illustrations used. Each chapter is complete in itself and contains spiritual truth, as well as intellectual assistance towards a mastery of theology and the preparation for external examinations. Theology divorced from experience or Scripture can be a soul-destroying process, but when related to both can be a means of grace. We do not need Schleiermacher (a twentieth-century German theologian of liberal thought) to stress for us the importance of relating doctrine to feeling. No apology therefore is made for notes that occur from time to time relating to experience.

Two shifts of gravity have taken place in Theology during the last few decades. The first is to make central a study of the Person of Christ rather than the Church and Sacraments. This is logical and good. Newton's lines hold true here:

What think you of Christ? is the test to try both yourself and your scheme,
You cannot be right in the rest, unless you think rightly of Him.

The second development, astonishing at first sight, though naturally following from the influence of Barth, has occurred within current Christology itself. The change is this: where once the Jesus of History was accepted as fact, and the Christ of Experience rejected as fiction, there is a trend today to regard the Jesus of History as myth and the Christ of Experience—for those who accept Him—as real. This surely is a far more dangerous thrust for it divorces Christianity from Historic Reality. The old liberalism razed the castle, but left the foundations of Christology firmly embedded in the rock of historic fact. The modern trend destroys these foundations, but affects to leave the castle entire, floating in mid-air. But what happens to such castles?—This new challenge I have endeavoured to face squarely.

In the last analysis most of the modern attacks upon the Bible doctrine of our Lord seek to drive a wedge between the realities which evangelical Christians believe to be identical—the Jesus of History who walked the shores of the Sea of Galilee, the Christ of Experience worshipped by the Church in Acts and in the twentieth century, and the Christ of the Creeds (of Nicea, of the Westminster Confession, the Augsburg Symbols, the Thirty-nine Articles). This series has as its aim the identifying of these realities in clearly marked stages.

The Authorized Version, corrected where necessary, has been followed throughout, for a number of reasons. No other version has the same hold upon the affections and memory of the English-speaking peoples, endeared as it is by early associations and familiarized by exclusive use in literature; no other version remains an invariable standard, all the other translations in due course giving place to yet others; finally, no other version is made accessible by having all the great concordances based upon it.

This work is designed for students, and for the sake of brevity and clearness the synoptic style of writing and of typography has been largely followed.

Sets of Advanced Questions appear at the end of each chapter which are based on and answered by the contents of the next. The present Series sets out to do more than merely present Biblical Theology in assimilable form. It is prepared to help even immature Christians to draw doctrine from Scripture for themselves. It is further designed to serve as an instrument in the hands of experienced leaders both in this land and in new countries, to draw out the native abilities of national workers in training, to develop initiative in thinking and maturity in judgment, assisting them to form for themselves from Scripture an authentic system of Christian doctrine.

A list of some of the books that have been consulted, or that are recommended for B.D. and Dip.Theol. work appears separately. Generally speaking acknowledgment has been given in the text where conscious reference has been made. I am indebted to Bevil Browne's splendid little volume, *The Way and the Life*, for an interesting historical allusion in Chapter Four.

As to the history of the present book, some twenty years ago the earlier chapters were circulated as a Correspondence Course, in another form, and the author still possesses valued sheaves of typescript drafts heavily worked over by the saintly E. J. Poole-Connor in his fatherly concern for accuracy of detail. Almost all, however, has been rewritten for this volume. The material of these studies, incidentally, has been given since 1938 almost without interruption in its place in a three-year cycle in lectures given twice weekly in four different Bible Colleges, so that what is written is based on experience of the need of students and teacher alike. It represents, with a certain building-up of material, eight lectures in this cycle.

But for the faith and sacrifice of two members of our secretarial staff, who wish to remain anonymous, this volume would, humanly speaking, never have been written. Their vision and prayerfulness have stimulated the work in the first place, and when it was undertaken they proved indefatigable co-operators, handling in their spare time the work of typing and checking the manuscripts.

I pray that God who I believe guided and enabled me in its production will use it to help Christians everywhere, and especially those preparing for the work of the ministry, whether at home or overseas.

H. B. B.

February, 1967
The Birmingham Bible Institute,
Birmingham, 15, England.

TABLE OF CONTENTS IN SYNOPTIC FORM

ACKNOWLEDGMENTS

Permission has been kindly granted by the respective publishers to quote from the following works, for which I am grateful:

Biblical Theology; Vos, G.; W. B. Eerdmans Publishing Co.
In Understanding Be Men; Hammond, T. C.; Inter-Varsity Fellowship
Systematic Theology; Strong, A. H.; Judson Press
Teacher's Commentary on St. Matthew; Glover, R.; Marshall, Morgan & Scott

ADVANCE QUESTIONS ON CHAPTER ONE: STAGES IN THE REVELATION OF JESUS CHRIST

1. How were people saved in Old Testament times? Had the sacrifice of Christ upon the Cross any significance for them? If so, what? Can you give any Scripture to support your answer?

2. How do you explain the statement contained in Rev. 13. 8 that Christ is "the Lamb slain from the foundation of the world" when we all know He died about A.D. 30?

3. What is the earliest instance in the Bible of animal sacrifice as a means of atonement for sin? Can you draw any conclusions from this occasion and its date?

4. What did the lambs of the Old Testament represent to God? See John 1. 29, 36; 1 Cor. 5. 7; 1 Pet. 1. 18–20.

5. Is there any Scriptural warrant for saying that God *foreordained* the Fall? What doctrinal untruth would this entail if it were so? Could 1 Pet. 1. 18–20 be brought forward to support this view? Why?

6. Where did Christ in the Gospels refer to the fall of Satan before the world was made? Special reference may be made to John 8.

7. Can you think of any Old Testament prophecies that foretell that Christ should die? Of these, can you point out any that expressly state that the purpose of His death was to take away sins?

8. How would you explain Gen. 4. 7? "If thou doest well, shalt thou not be accepted? and if thou doest not well, sin lieth at the door. And unto thee shall be his desire, and thou shalt rule over him"? (This may give useful experience in looking up various commentaries.)

9. Did Christ die for *all men* or only for the *elect*? Give Scripture for your answer.

10. The Bible has a lot to say about the Blood of Sacrifices and about the Blood of Christ. Can you summarize its teaching? Include such Scripture as Lev. 17. 11; Heb. 9. 22; 10. 4; 1 Pet. 1. 18–20.

11. Is it true to say with Mary Baker Eddy, the founder of Christian Science, that "the blood of Jesus was of no more avail when shed than when in His veins"? Why? Give Scripture for your answer.

12. In the book of Acts we frequently read such statements as "They preached the Word", "So mightily grew the Word of God and prevailed". What is this "Word"? Is it the Old Testament? Is it the New Testament? Is it something else?

CHAPTER ONE

STAGES IN THE REVELATION OF JESUS CHRIST

THE stages in the revelation of our Lord Jesus Christ may be compared to those in the construction of a *battleship*. In the latter there are four stages.

1. There is first the *decision* that a vessel of a certain tonnage, draught, dimensions, armament and materials shall be constructed.
2. There follows the production of *scale-drawings* in large quantities, accurately depicting the ship as a whole, and in detail.
3. Next, a *scale-model* of the ship is prepared at immense cost. This is tested under conditions of great secrecy in a private basin.
4. Finally, the *vessel* itself is constructed, according to plans and model.

Similarly, in the redemption of the world through the revelation of Jesus Christ there were four stages:

1. There was God's *decision* before the world began that man should be redeemed by the Incarnation of His Son, and His atoning Death.
2. There was the announcement of this decision, and the production of His plan of Redemption by means of innumerable prophecies in the Old Testament, which correspond to the *scale-drawings*.
3. His work of Redemption was symbolized to the Old Testament saints by means of types. These might be people, buildings, religious ceremonies or historical incidents, all setting forth some aspect of Christ's person or work. These answer to the *scale-models*.
4. Finally, the work of Redemption was actually accomplished by the Birth, Death, Resurrection and Ascension of our Lord.

We are now to examine these Four Stages:

1. THE DIVINE DECISION

1. THE PERSONS DECIDING: THE HOLY TRINITY

God is a Trinity of Three Persons in one Godhead, the Father, the Son and the Holy Spirit. This Three-in-Oneness has existed from eternity. Before ever the Son became Man, He was co-equal, co-eternal and consubstantial with the Father and the Spirit. (This doctrine is more fully dealt with in Chapter Three.) It was the Three Persons of the Godhead who decreed Redemption.

2. THE DIVINE FOREKNOWLEDGE OF THE FALL OF MAN

The Bible teaches that the fall of Satan, an archangel, with certain other angels, took place before the world was made. Christ described this fall in John 8.44. He said, "He was a murderer from the beginning, and abode not in the truth."

It would seem that Satan, thus cast out of heaven, sought to secure possession of the world at its creation, and of man who was made by God to enjoy fellowship with Himself, and to bear rule over the lesser creation. In order to injure God, and to gain control of His world, Satan induced man to sin (as described in Gen. 3) who thus became a fallen being. He was alienated from God, his spirit died, his soul was blinded and perverted, his body made liable to disease and death, and the moral malady called sin entered the blood-stream of the human race. Thus man passed under the usurped control of the devil, or Satan (cp. Acts 26. 18; Col. 1. 13; Heb. 2. 14).

It was in order to redeem man from the guilt and power of sin, to restore him, not only to his former position but to one far higher, that God's plan of Redemption was determined upon. It would be costly, as "the wages of sin is death" (Rom. 6. 23).

God provided that the penalty should be paid by the only One who was able to pay it, His own Son. He would take human nature "that through death He might destroy him that had the power of death, that is, the devil" (Heb. 2. 14).

At the core of certain types of rope there is always a scarlet thread. Wherever it is cut, the scarlet thread will be seen. In a similar way the scarlet thread of Redemption runs through the Bible.

While it is plain from Scripture that God *foreknew* that the Fall of Man would occur, it must never be thought that God *foreordained* it. This would be to regard God as the author of sin, and as morally responsible for all the effects of it. He *foreknew* the Fall; but He *foreordained* Redemption. The difference between the two words may be made clearer by an illustration. Some years ago the Perth to London Express was travelling near the Boxmoor Tunnel at seventy m.p.h. just before diversion from the fast to the slow line. These points should have been taken at fifteen m.p.h. The train consequently left the rails and plunged over the embankment. As a result over forty people lost their lives. At the enquiry the signalman stated that he observed the train running too rapidly for safety and testified, "*I saw it would happen.*" He *foreknew* there would be a train-wreck but he did not foreordain it; indeed, he did all in his power to avert it. It was so with God in relation to the Fall of Man. Why He did not prevent it is a problem which the Bible does not explain. We can only take facts as we find them, and as the Bible states them to be—that is, that God's creature, Man, has fallen, and that he has been redeemed. Until we have clearer light we must trust where we cannot trace.

3. GOD'S FOREORDINATION OF REDEMPTION

Because God foreknew the Fall He foreordained man's Redemption. Provision of a stretcher and remedies in the event of an accident does not bring about an accident. It was not *lest* man should fall; God knew that he *would*. Conceivably, Adam, and mankind in Adam, did not need to fall; but when he did so, God's plan of Redemption was ready and was announced to him before his doom was declared. This foreordination of Redemption from before the foundation of the world answers to the decision that a battleship (see Section 1) should be built. That it was decreed prior to the Fall is plain from the following: 1 Pet. 1. 18–20 says, "Ye were not redeemed with corruptible things, as silver and gold. . . . but with the precious blood of Christ, as of a lamb without blemish and without spot: who verily was foreordained [Greek *pro-ginōskō*, to know before, hence fore-known] before the foundation of the world". Rev. 13. 8, referring to Christ, speaks of the "book of life of the Lamb slain from the foundation of the world".

NOTE: These two verses, especially the latter, raise some questions. If Christ died on the Passover Preparation Day, A.D. 30, how could He be said to die before the foundation of the world? Did He die twice? Could He die before He became man? The answer is that He was slain before the foundation of the world not in point of time, but in the intents and purposes of the Triune God. Two considerations will make this clear.

1. With man, willing and doing are two different things. Man often wills what he is unable to perform; or he may change his mind later. God, being omnipotent, is never unable to carry out what He purposes (Rom. 4. 21); and because He is unchangeable His plans never alter. With Him to will and to do are identical, however far apart in time the decision and action may be.

2. With God, the past, present and future are an eternally present NOW. A canoeist on a winding river sees only his particular reach of the stream; an airman, looking down from his 'plane,

sees with equal clearness where the canoeist has been and where he is going. To the Holy Trinity the Cross was eternally present, for God's foreknowledge of the event caused it to be as near and as real before the beginning of the world as in the moment of time when it actually took place. All this explains, as seen in a later chapter, how God could forgive sin in Old Testament times on the ground of the yet future sacrifice of Christ.

2. THE "SCALE-DRAWINGS" OF OLD TESTAMENT PROPHECIES

These will be referred to in detail in a later volume. Three prophecies will here be mentioned. After the Fall God spoke to the serpent (Satan or His tool) thus, "I will put enmity between thee and the woman, and between thy seed and her seed; it shall bruise thy head, and thou shalt bruise his heel" (Gen. 3. 15).

The seed of the serpent represents those who, animated by the Evil One, put Christ to death (John 8. 44); the Seed of the woman is Christ; the bruising of His heel by the serpent is His Crucifixion; the bruising of Satan's head by Christ is his defeat at the Cross (Col. 2. 14–15) and his ultimate destruction.

Before God *pronounced* the penalty of sin upon the woman and the man, He *announced* their redemption, according to His eternally decided plan.

Isa. 53. 4–6 reads, "He [i.e. the Messiah, meaning Christ] hath borne our griefs, and carried our sorrows: yet we did esteem him stricken, smitten of God, and afflicted. But he was wounded for our transgressions, he was bruised for our iniquities: the chastisement of our peace was upon him; and with his stripes we are healed. All we like sheep have gone astray; we have turned every one to his own way; and the Lord hath laid on him the iniquity of us all."

Here we see One, that is, Christ, who was to be born, to take the form of a servant, and to die, not for His own sin, but as bearing the sins of all who have gone astray.

Psa. 16. 10 is another prophecy or "scale-drawing" of the Resurrection of Christ (cp. Acts 2. 25–31). It reads, "Thou [i.e. God the Father] wilt not leave my soul [i.e. the Messiah's] in hell [Hebrew, *sheol* = Greek, *Hades*, the unseen world of spirits that have departed]; neither wilt thou suffer thine Holy One to see corruption."

3. THE "SCALE-MODEL" OF OLD TESTAMENT TYPES

Between the Fall of Man and the Coming of Christ God was pleased to reveal His purpose of redemption not only by prophecy but by symbol. He used the picture-language of material objects and the symbolism of action. Of the many types of Christ in the Old Testament none is older or clearer than that of the sacrificial lamb.

Adam's son, Abel, evidently realized that he was a sinner and offered a lamb which was accepted by God. Who told him to do this? It can have been none other than God in the revelation which He made to Adam. It was repeated to Cain when the latter was angry that his brother's sacrifice had been accepted and his own rejected. God said to him, "If thou doest well, shalt thou not be accepted? and if thou doest not well, a *Sin-Offering* lieth at the door" (Gen. 4. 7). The Hebrew word *chattah* means either "sin" or "sin-offering"; the latter should obviously be used here. Instead of slaying the lamb, Cain slew his brother.

Thus from the first generation God taught men that His Son would one day become a Sacrifice for sin. This divine revelation was handed down among the races of mankind, often by tradition which was preserved in a garbled and perverted form. It was restored to Israel in purity and accuracy in the law of Moses. The sacrificial lambs therein prescribed for sacrifice were all types and symbols of the Lord Jesus Christ, who was yet to give "himself a ransom for all" (1 Tim. 2. 6). Through these lambs God's people were able to exercise faith in Him of whom they were the symbols. The Altar of Judaism sets forth the Cross of Christianity. Before Christ came, men were saved through grace by faith in a *prophetic* or future sacrifice; after He came they were saved through grace by faith in an *historic* or past sacrifice, *but it is in each case one and the same sacrifice.* There never was a time when men were saved otherwise than through grace by faith in the sacrifice for all mankind made by Jesus Christ. This is a pivotal point in Scripture and cannot be too strongly insisted upon.

Some years ago an Englishman was accused of spying at a fort in Cuba, and sentenced to death. The British and American Consuls, convinced of his innocence, appeared at the time fixed for his execution and draped the British and American flags around him saying in effect, "Fire, if you dare!" The muskets were lowered, and eventually the man was released. Could coloured bunting protect a man against bullets? Only when it was a symbol of that which was greater than itself—the authority and power of two great countries. So in Old Testament times, it was not the mere blood of bulls or goats that saved; Heb. 10. 4 says of the inefficacy of these, "It is not possible that the blood of bulls and of goats should take away sins." What removes sins is that of which it was the symbol, that is, the blood of Christ.

Lev. 17. 11 says, "The life of the flesh is in the blood: and I have given it to you upon the altar to make an atonement for your souls:

for it is the blood that maketh an atonement for the soul." There is no other basis for the remission of sins apart from blood atonement. Heb. 9. 22 says, "Without shedding of blood is no remission."

Blood does not merely mean *life*, but life *poured out in death*. Sir Robert Anderson, a former Chief of Scotland Yard, says in reference to this subject, that when he had to examine the scene of the terrible Whitechapel murders, the work of "Jack the Ripper", he found blood everywhere, which spoke to him not of life but of death. So in Scripture the blood of Christ means the death of Christ. It is untrue to say that His blood, when shed, was of no more avail than when it was in His veins. *In all Mosaic sacrifices the victim had to die before its blood became efficacious.*

The value of blood depends upon the value of the being in whose veins it runs. The worth of the blood of Christ is infinite, because He is infinite. This will all be touched on later. The plan of the Incarnation cannot be separated from that of Redemption (Heb. 2. 14) and the Redemption in turn is impossible without the Incarnation.

4. THE FULFILMENT OF PROPHECY AND TYPE IN THE COMING OF THE LORD JESUS CHRIST

The four Gospels record the Birth, Death, Resurrection and Ascension of Christ. They are a record of the fulfilment of that which God revealed in prophecy and type in the Old Testament. The older Scriptures pointed *forward* to Christ; our Lord when on earth pointed to or revealed Himself (cp. John 4. 26; 9. 35–38); the apostles pointed *backward* to the historic Christ, giving witness of His Resurrection.

The Book of Acts records their testimony, and is a history of the spread of "the word". The phrase "word of God" or "the word of the Lord" occurs constantly throughout this book always in such language as this, "They spake unto him (the Philippian jailer) the word of the Lord, and to all that were in his house" (Acts 16. 32); "The word of God was preached of Paul at Berea" (Acts 17. 13); "He continued there (in Corinth) a year and six months, teaching the word of God among them" (Acts 18. 11); "So mightily grew the word of God and prevailed" (Acts 19. 20).

The "word of the Lord" which the apostles preached was not (1) the Old Testament, though this was constantly quoted, nor (2) the New Testament, which was not then written, but (3) simply the Gospel. Heb. 2. 3 tells us that it was the continuation of the same Word which the Lord preached while on earth, which was Himself. The Gospel which they preached was first to last, Christ, that is, the facts of His Incarnation, His atoning Death, His physical Resurrection, His Ascension and His Coming Again, and all as fulfilling the Old Testament prophecies. It was what the theologians would call a "Christology" or "Word about Christ". With these facts and this interpretation they proclaimed two other doctrines: the first was that the twofold *response* to the Gospel that God requires, is repentance towards Himself and faith towards the Lord Jesus Christ (see Acts 20. 21). By repentance was meant turning to God from sin, and by faith the act of the will in accepting Jesus Christ's death as the ground of acceptance with God. Faith so definitely involved Repentance that often the latter was omitted and only Faith mentioned (cp. Acts 16. 30, 31). The second doctrine was that, when men made this response to the "Christology", God responded by giving them remission of sins, a new heart, His Holy Spirit, and spiritual blessings. The record in the Acts of the Apostles confirms the truth of this; and later experience shows that when these historic facts of His Incarnation, Death, Resurrection, Ascension and Coming Again are preached "according to the scriptures" (1 Cor. 15. 3, 4), and the conditions of repentance and faith stated, God blesses it with results similar to those therein related.

NOTE: The Second Coming of Christ is above referred to as an "historic fact" although still future. But as Christ was said to be "slain from the foundation of the world" and His death was therefore to God an eternal fact, His Second Coming is so essential to the divine purpose as to be similarly regarded. A brief examination of the Acts of the Apostles will bear out the above statements in regard to the preaching of the Gospel.

There are thirty-five different proclamations of the "Word" in this portion of Scripture. The first, Acts 2. 14–40, may be taken as a sample.

1. THE CHRISTOLOGY GIVEN

Peter implies Christ's *deity* in verse 27, where he calls Him God's "Holy One", which, in the setting of Messianic prophecy, has this force. He dwells on His *death* in vv. 23 and 36 and states that He was "delivered by the determinate counsel and foreknowledge of God." He refers to His *Resurrection* in vv. 30–32, asserting, "This Jesus hath God raised up, whereof we all are witnesses." He announces His *Ascension* in vv. 33–36, "Being by the right hand of God exalted, and having received of the Father the promise of the Holy Ghost, he hath shed forth this, which ye now see and hear. For David is not ascended into the heavens: but he saith himself The Lord said unto my Lord, Sit Thou on my right hand, Until I make thy foes thy footstool. Therefore let all the house of Israel know assuredly, that God hath made that same Jesus, whom ye crucified, both Lord and Christ." The *Second Coming* of Christ is not proclaimed by Peter in this sermon, but it is in his next, when he says, "He shall send Jesus Christ, which before was preached unto you" (Acts 3. 20, 21; cp. Paul, in Acts 17. 32).

2. THE RESPONSE REQUIRED

Coming now to the *Response* required, Peter when his hearers asked him, "What shall we do?" replied, "Repent, and be baptized every one of you in the name of Jesus Christ for the remission of sins" (Acts 2. 37, 38). Baptism is the seal and culmination of faith and hence implies it. To Cornelius in Acts 10. 43 Peter says, "Through his name whosoever believeth in him shall receive remission of sins." Paul, in Acts 13. 38, 39, says, "Through this man is preached unto you the forgiveness of sins: and by him *all that believe* are justified from all things, from which ye could not be justified by the law of Moses."

3. THE RESULTS PROMISED

The third part of the passage deals with the promises. These are:

(1) "The remission of sins" (Acts 2. 38; cp. 10. 43; 13. 38, 39).

(2) "The gift of the Holy Ghost" (Acts 2. 38, 39; 3. 19; cp. 5. 31, 32; 10. 43, 44).

(3) Salvation: e.g. to the Philippian jailer Paul said, "Believe on the Lord Jesus Christ, and thou shalt be *saved*" (Acts 16. 31).

NOTES

NOTES

ADVANCE QUESTIONS ON CHAPTER TWO: THE VIRGIN BIRTH

THE reader who wishes to be also a student of the Bible is invited not to rush into the next chapter right away, but first of all to pause and to think for himself about its subject. What one digs out for oneself is more valuable than what is merely shovelled in by another. It has personal worth, for the truth is part of oneself. As such it can far more naturally be passed on to others.

The following questions are given for those who wish to do private or group Bible Study. They all relate to the subject dealt with in the next chapter, and will be answered by reading it. Accordingly they may be termed "Self-Correcting Exercises". As with the questions preceding the first chapter they will be given *before* this and each chapter, to assist students of the Word to study it and to think for themselves. Maturity of spiritual judgment, a sense of utter dependence upon the Word of God rather than the words of men, an ability to feed on that Word, and great personal blessing are results to be expected. If the private study can be undertaken in connection with a Bible Class the value and interest of the work there will be increased greatly.

These questions are not all easy and may cause you some perplexity. If this is so, there are two courses you may follow. First of all you may look over the following list and only tackle those you think you can handle. Second, you may divide your group into, say, three or four teams the week before and during the week make each group responsible for tackling a third or a quarter of the questions.

Again, students may be assigned to work at these in pairs.

When the day arrives a wise leader will encourage the members by skilful cross-questioning to share with the others what they have learned, to draw out the diffident, and to give them confidence in speaking in public; to correct any wrong deductions, and to help each one feel that he is part of the team and has made a real contribution.

The simplest way to use these questions is to distribute them at the close of the preceding lesson, which gives everyone one week to prepare. Either before or after the next week's lesson is given he holds a forum, collecting and collating the various findings of the members. It is important that before the class is dismissed a general agreement on all vital points should be reached, with at least an "agreement to differ" on the rest.

1. Some people hold that the Virgin Birth as a doctrine is not important. It is quite immaterial, say they, whether we believe it or not. Is this correct? Give full reasons for your answer.

2. Where in the Bible is there a reference to the Virgin Birth? Can you include in this list any references in the Old Testament?

3. The Roman Catholics and certain High Churchmen believe in what is called the Perpetual Virginity of Mary. How could you refute this from Scripture?

4. There are two genealogies of our Lord in the New Testament, one in Matt. 1 and the other in Luke 3. (1) Are they identical? (2) If not, wherein do they differ? (3) Can you give a reason for this?

5. Read carefully the closing verses of Jer. 22. Can you see any connection between these verses and the difference in the genealogies?

6. In the two genealogies from David to Christ there are two or three identical names. What are they? Read Hag. 2. 23. Does this verse provide any explanation?

7. In what other respects does the Roman Catholic doctrine about the Virgin Mary differ from that held by Protestants? Why do the latter think they are right? Give Scripture in each case.

8. What useful ministry did Joseph perform in the life of the Holy Family?

9. What useful purpose in connection with the Virgin Birth was served by Elisabeth's childlessness and the subsequent answer to her prayers (Luke 1. 5–40)?

CHAPTER TWO

THE VIRGIN BIRTH

By the term "the Virgin Birth" we mean that Jesus Christ was "conceived by the Holy Ghost, born of the Virgin Mary." We also understand that His was different from ordinary births, as in these there is the creation at birth of a new personality but His involved a pre-existing personality entering upon a new stage.

In this chapter we consider the importance of five factors related to it:

1. The Virgin Birth itself.
2. The Virgin Mary
3. The Holy Spirit
4. Joseph
5. The Genealogies

1. THE IMPORTANCE OF THE VIRGIN BIRTH

Some say it is unimportant whether or not we believe the doctrine of the Virgin Birth, and that one can deny it and still be a Christian. It is further asserted that only two Scriptures in the New Testament—Matt. 1. 18 and Luke 1. 34, 35—and one in the Old Testament—Isa. 7. 14—refer to it, that Paul and John know nothing of the doctrine, and thus a subject which the Bible deals with so scantily cannot be of vital Christian importance.

The reply to this is as follows:

1. EXPLANATION OF INCARNATION

The doctrine of the Virgin Birth is of fundamental importance because only thus can it be explained how God, the Second Person in the Trinity, became Man, and took human nature into eternal union with His divine nature. No one ever yet denied the Virgin Birth and found himself able to accept the New Testament doctrine of the Person of Christ. The two stand or fall together.

2. SAFEGUARD OF SINLESSNESS

If the Virgin Birth be denied we have no ground for belief in the sinlessness of our Lord, nor even in the legitimacy of His Birth.

3. MANUSCRIPT AUTHORITY

The two passages in the New Testament in which the doctrine of the Virgin Birth is clearly taught are of great importance. These are Matt. 1. 18 and Luke 1. 34–35. Their place in the original text is above reasonable doubt. Practically every single manuscript has them except a mutilated manuscript of the Ebionites (a Jewish–Christian sect which denied Christ's deity) who excised many things that spoke of this fact. There is also one Syriac reading of Matt. 1. 18 which is certainly wrong: it says that Joseph begat Jesus, but the narrative even here goes on to narrate the Virgin Birth. The early editions of Moffatt's Modern English Translation following Von Soden's text rendered this accordingly. Dr. G. Campbell Morgan when ministering in the United States once came on a pulpit edition of this Testament in which he had to read this for his lesson. He shut up the book and slammed it down with the words, "Enough of this blasphemy!"

The other passage, Luke 1. 34–35 was written by Paul's intimate companion, Luke the beloved Physician (see Col. 4. 14; 2 Tim. 4. 11; Philem. 24) who states in his introduction that he describes "those things which are most surely believed among us" (Luke 1. 1–4). It is therefore impossible that Paul, with whom he was so closely associated, even to the last days of his life (2 Tim. 4. 11) should have been ignorant of this vital belief.

4. UNIVERSAL IMPLICATION IN THE NEW TESTAMENT

The doctrine of the Virgin Birth, though only twice specifically mentioned in the New Testament, is clearly implied throughout. It is in this respect similar to the doctrine of the Trinity, which also is everywhere implied in the Bible, but nowhere expressly stated. (The passage in 1 John 5. 7 is not found in any reliable Greek manuscript and is rightly omitted from the Revised Version.) Paul, for example, believes at one and the same time in the real human birth of our Lord and in His deity. Thus in Rom. 1. 3–4 he says that Christ is "*made of the seed of David according to the flesh*" yet "declared to be the Son of God with power, according to the spirit of holiness, by the resurrection from the dead", and in Gal. 4. 4 that "God sent forth his Son, *made of a woman, made under the law*". In 2 Tim. 2. 8 Paul reiterates his doctrinal position formally: "Remember that Jesus Christ *of the seed of David* was raised from the dead according to my gospel." The writer of Hebrews affirms, "Forasmuch then as the children are partakers *of flesh and blood, he also himself likewise took part of the same*" (2. 14) and "*took on him the seed of Abraham*" (2. 16).

Mark omits the Virgin Birth but too much need not be implied by this. It does not fall within his plan.

John the Evangelist is silent about the Virgin Birth, it is true, but he is silent about a lot of other things, such as the Temptation and the Transfiguration. He does not repeat facts already well-known, nor details supplied by the other three evangelists who laid down their pens thirty to forty years before he took up his. He implies his hearers understand all about baptism, and even his doctrine of the Logos, or Word. He enlarges only on aspects of Christ's earthly life that he has pre-selected to prove his thesis: "That Jesus is the Messiah (or Christ) the Son of God" (John 20. 31). Nevertheless, John clearly stresses the facts of Christ's genuine humanity and His absolute deity, twin columns of a vast arch that imply one common foundation beneath them—the Virgin Birth. Read carefully John 1. 14; 1 John 1. 2; 4. 2, 3; 5. 6. R. V. says, "The Word became *flesh*" (John 1. 14).

It would seem that these and other early writers of the first or second centuries omit reference to the Virgin Birth because as all believed and accepted it in the church there was no need to defend it. Men only defend a thing when it is attacked from the outside. In many a fundamentalist church in America and Britain the Virgin Birth is not preached on or even mentioned for years on end. It is simply assumed without question.

5. UNIVERSAL ACCEPTANCE IN THE EARLY CHURCH

To document this fact we have the testimony of the Apostles' Creed which says that Christ was "conceived by the Holy Ghost, born of the Virgin Mary." Our form of the creed is the Gallican of the fifth or sixth centuries which is based on the Old Roman baptismal formula of A.D. 200 which is nearly the same throughout and is practically identical where it deals with the Virgin Birth. This reads "born of the Holy Ghost and the Virgin Mary" (instead of "conceived by the Virgin Mary").

First of all this proves that it was an integral part of the belief of the Roman Church and confessed by every convert before baptism. The fact that the Creed was used as a baptismal formula, which is a stereotyped thing, implies that it had for long previously been an essential part of everybody's accepted doctrine. A creed is simply crystallized belief, and crystallization takes time.

Actually the date of A.D. 170–250 is the latest normally given to this formula, but as both Justin Martyr (died A.D. 165) and Ignatius quote it as an accepted Creed, this implies A.D. 100 as the more probable date. Ignatius, who died not later than A.D. 117 mentions the Virgin Birth very clearly in several passages and regards the virginity of Mary as one "of the mysteries to be shouted aloud"—i.e. one of the mysteries which was prepared by God in silence but now proclaimed for the ages by the wondrous star of the heavens. Ignatius was a bishop not a novice, and his memory would stretch far back into apostolic times.

Secondly, the character of the Apostles' Creed is such that it contains only the barest necessities, especially regarding Christ, so that we see the Virgin Birth practically from the first was reckoned as among the essentials of the faith.

Thirdly, the Roman Church was central in the old world so that which was its belief, was doubtless that of the church at large.

These circumstances combine to prove that belief in the Virgin Birth must have prevailed universally long before the close of the first century. (For further study see Machen's *Virgin Birth.*)

2. THE IMPORTANCE OF THE VIRGIN MARY

1. THE HUMANITY OF THE VIRGIN MARY

The Virgin Mary was not different in herself from any other woman, but was one who "rejoices" in God her Saviour (Luke 1. 47). She was a sinner as truly as any other woman and saved by grace through faith in the atoning work of the Son, like others. She was a Jewess of the lineage of David through his son, Nathan, and was chosen to be the privileged instrument whereby the Second Person of the Godhead should lay hold of humanity and permanently unite human nature with His divine nature. Mary's blood, but not Joseph's, flowed in His veins. The lineaments of Mary's face would doubtless show in His own. Our Saviour was a Jew.

2. THE FAITH OF THE VIRGIN MARY

The Virgin Birth was a divinely wrought miracle and, as in practically all other miracles, while it was wholly a work of God, man (or woman) had a conditioning part to play. That part was faith. Mary had to believe God for something different from and more wonderful than anything that had ever happened in history. That was why God allowed Elisabeth, her cousin, to go through years of frustration ending in hopelessness as to ever having a baby, and at the very last to find God miraculously answered her prayers. It was to give the Virgin Mary faith for her greater miracle. That was why the angel told her to see Elisabeth at once, for the same God that wrought the lesser wonder would now work the greater (Luke 1. 36, 37) and upon this announcement (or "Annunciation" as it is called) (Luke 1. 26, 38) Mary "believed" (Luke 1. 45).

3. THE SCRIPTURES CONCERNING THE VIRGIN MARY

(1) Matt. 1. 18–25 contains the following statements: "Now the birth of Jesus Christ was on this wise: When as his mother Mary was espoused to Joseph, before they came together, she was found with child of the Holy Ghost." The angel of the Lord said, "Joseph, thou son of David, fear not to take unto thee Mary thy wife: for that which is conceived in her is of the Holy Ghost . . . Now all this was done, that it might be fulfilled which was spoken of the Lord by the prophet, saying, Behold, a virgin (Greek, *parthenos*) shall be with child, and shall bring forth a son, and they shall call his name Emmanuel, which being interpreted is, God with us . . . Joseph . . . knew her not till she had brought forth her firstborn son: and he called his name Jesus."

(2) Luke 1. 30–35 reads in part, "The angel said . . . Fear not, Mary . . . thou shalt conceive in thy womb, and bring forth a son, and shalt call his name Jesus. He shall be great, and shall be called the Son of the Highest; and the Lord God shall give unto him the throne of his father David: And he shall reign over the house of Jacob for ever; and of his kingdom there shall be no end. Then said Mary unto the angel, How shall this be, seeing I know not a man? And the angel answered and said unto her, The Holy Ghost shall come upon thee, and the power of the Highest shall overshadow thee: therefore also that holy thing which shall be born of thee shall be called the Son of God."

(3) The Scripture quoted in Matt. 1 is from Isa. 7. 10–19, part of which speaks thus: "The Lord spake again unto Ahaz, saying, Ask thee a sign of the Lord thy God; ask it either in the depth, or in the height above. But Ahaz said, I will not ask, neither will I tempt the Lord. And he (Isaiah speaking for God) said . . . Therefore the Lord himself shall give you a sign; Behold, a virgin shall conceive, and bear a son, and shall call his name Immanuel . . . Before the child shall know to refuse the evil, and choose the good, the land that thou abhorrest (Northern Israel with Syria) shall be forsaken of both her kings. The Lord shall bring upon thee . . . even the king of Assyria . . . And they shall come."

The historical picture is that of Isaiah told by God to meet King Ahaz of Jerusalem just outside the city at the fountain which he was planning to divert and seal up against an invasion by his enemies, the axis formed by the coalition of Northern Israel and Syria. To ward off this invasion he contemplated calling Assyria to his aid. It was as if to defend himself against two fierce little puppies a man should call in a wolf (Isa. 7. 1–9). God told him through Isaiah not to do this for He Himself would save Judah, and He promised that, to strengthen his faith, He would grant any sign he asked (Isa. 7. 11, 12). Ahaz refused because he was determined not to trust God (v. 12). Isaiah then said God Himself would give him a sign. A virgin (Hebrew, *almah*, an unmarried woman) would bear a son and before he could cry "My father" or "My mother", i.e. before he was three years old, the coalition would be overthrown by Assyria (Isa. 8. 1–4 and cp. 8. 8–10 remembering that Immanuel means "God with us"). The prophecy has thus, as is the case so often in Scripture, a double fulfilment, one near at hand and one distant. The distant, prophetic fulfilment of which the near one was but shadow and foretaste and type, was in Christ, and the *almah* was the Virgin Mary. But there was also an immediate typical fulfilment—for a birth over 700 years later would have no significance to Ahaz in the present emergency. This near fulfilment was in the birth of Maher-shal-al-hash-baz (Isa. 8. 1) the prophet's second son, and his mother was Isaiah's wife, herself a prophetess (Isa. 8. 1–3) the birth taking place shortly after the interview with Ahaz.

Almah usually, though not invariably, signifies a virgin, a young unmarried woman. It was translated by the Septuagint, the Greek Version of the Old Testament, by the uncompromising word *parthenos* which can have only one meaning and nothing else—virgin. The Septuagint was the Jews' "Authorized Version" till the first century, and the Christians' at all times. As the Christians used the word *parthenos* to defend the Virgin Birth and made the Septuagint generally their Bible and, as the Hebrew text itself was undergoing revision, the Jews lost all interest in it and had a succession of other translations into Greek, e.g. those of Aquila, Symmachus and Theodotion, in which *almah* was translated not by *parthenos* but *neanis*, a young woman, presumably, but not inevitably, unmarried.

4. THE FIVE POPULAR ERRORS CONCERNING THE VIRGIN MARY

(1) **Mariolatry** (from *Maria* and *latreia*, worship—i.e. the worship of the Virgin Mary). When during the reign of the Roman Emperor Constantine in the fourth century, Christianity became the State religion, a tendency to deify the Virgin Mary developed, i.e. to raise her to the rank of a goddess to be worshipped. She began to be called the "Mother of God", which is quite untrue and blasphemous. Scholars have shown us how the Roman Church often permitted converted pagans to continue the adoration of their old deities under new names: in this case, that which had been given to certain goddesses was transferred to the Virgin Mary. Scripture knows nothing of such teaching. (Read Matt. 12. 46–50; John 2. 4, 5; cp. Acts 1. 14.) We should be careful while truly honouring the memory of

Mary, not to give her a place which Christ did not give her, and which belongs to the Godhead alone.

(2) **Immaculate Conception of the Virgin Mary.** One must not fall into the common error of applying this phrase to the sinless birth of Christ. It is a technical term which only applies to Mary's birth. It is the doctrine that she was born wholly without taint of original sin, a clumsy attempt to explain how our Lord in turn could have been born without taint of corruption or tendency to sin. Original Sin is the name given to that "want to" in relation to what is wrong, that predisposition to sin that is in the bloodstream of everyone. David truly says, "Behold, I was shapen in iniquity; and in sin did my mother conceive me" (Psa. 51. 5).

At the Roman Catholic Council of Trent in the sixteenth century the Pope, Paul III, pronounced an *anathema* against anyone who asserted that the Virgin was born immaculate, and against anyone who denied it. The Church was near to splitting into two parts because one section held one, and the other the contrary doctrine, so to avoid this disaster they shelved the question. This was taken from the shelf and settled officially once and for ever on 8th December, 1854.

There was a splendid service in St. Peter's, Rome. The place was packed. Surrounding the papal throne (cathedra) were five hundred mitred prelates. On the throne sat Pope Pius IX, arrayed in his red and white vestments of silk and damask, and his triple crown of gold and diamonds on his head.

There was an awe-inspiring silence of some minutes, and then a Cardinal clothed in purple, approached his Holiness, knelt, then prostrated himself before him and implored, "Holy Father, tell us if we can believe and teach that the Mother of God, the Holy Virgin Mary, was immaculate in her conception?"

Answered Pope Pius, "I do not know; let us ask the light of the Holy Ghost." He then knelt, and the vast throng with him, while the sweet-toned choir raised the strains of the "Veni Creator Spiritus". Hardly had the last echoes faded when the purple-clad Cardinal again threw himself before the Pontiff and asked the same question to receive the same response.

Again the anthem echoed round the sacred edifice.

A third time the poor Cardinal collected himself, stood before the Pope, knelt, then flung himself (really hard this time) and put the same question.

There was a pause; the Pope sat stock still; then suddenly, in a most awesome voice as if he had received a direct revelation from God, he made reply, "Yes! We must believe that the Blessed Virgin Mary, the Mother of God, was immaculate in her conception . . . There is no salvation to those who do not believe this dogma!" He thereupon with a loud voice chanted the "Te Deum", and, as if inspired by the news, three hundred peals of bells from as many churches in Rome rang out to herald it, while numerous cannons from the City thundered their applause.

This remarkable utterance of Pius IX is a good illustration of what is meant by the Pope saying anything *ex cathedra*, literally "from the papal throne", i.e. speaking officially as Pope. (This is now thought by Catholics to clinch any such statement as official catholic doctrine and finally authoritative.) From the moment of the Pope's announcement the Virgin Mary has been immaculate in her conception—at least in the belief of the Roman Catholic Church.

This is, of course, not true. As was said before, she was a sinner like the rest of us.

(3) **The Assumption of the Virgin Mary.** A similar act—though perhaps not quite so dramatically (or melodramatically) enacted occurred in 1952 when, under the above title, the Virgin was given a private Ascension to heaven (for that is what the Assumption really means).

(4) **The Intercession of the Virgin Mary.** In Roman Catholic doctrine the Virgin is seated beside Christ. To obtain the favour of the Father one must first win that of the Virgin, who assists in gaining that of the Son, then He reconciles you to the Father. All of this is quite ridiculous. If you were ill you would send for the doctor, not the doctor's mother. Christ said, "I am the way, the truth, and the life: no man cometh unto the Father, but by me" (John 14. 6) and Paul affirms in 1 Tim. 2. 5 that there is no other approach to the Father than that by Christ, and no other mediator, or middleman, either possible or necessary: "There is one God, and one mediator between God and men, the man Christ Jesus." Christ has a heart of infinite love to all of us and to say that man needs someone to placate Him, to secure His ever-ready ear, is an insult.

(5) **The Perpetual Virginity of the Virgin Mary.** Roman Catholics and high churchmen tend to teach that Mary was never married to Joseph after all, and her so-called sons are those of a cousin of hers. Scripture clearly teaches the reverse. As Richard Glover, in *The Gospel of Matthew*, p. 12, says, "The Saviour was reared in a *home*, not in a convent." His brothers and sisters are clearly mentioned in Matt. 13. 55–56. "Is not this the carpenter's son? is not his mother called Mary? and his brethren, James, and Joses, and Simon, and Judas? And his sisters, are they not all with us?" The word "all" implies that He had not less than three sisters. The Epistles of James and Jude were written by the brothers mentioned here.

Matt. 1. 25 says of the Virgin that Joseph "knew her not till she had brought forth her *firstborn* son", and this implies that afterwards she had a child or children by Joseph by natural generation. We are told much about these brethren. In Mark 3. 31 they attempt to see Him personally, quite probably to arrest Him (3. 21) for we read in John 7.5 that "neither did his brethren believe in him", which implies a stiffening of their attitude, for earlier they had accompanied Him with His mother and disciples to Capernaum (John 2. 12). Christ appeared to James after His resurrection and it was probably this meeting that converted him, so that afterwards he helped to lead the church in Jerusalem, and signed himself Christ's "bondslave" (James 1. 1—Greek *doulos* "servant"). All these facts indicate the normal married life of Mary after the Virgin Birth.

3. THE IMPORTANCE OF THE HOLY SPIRIT

The work of the Holy Spirit in the Birth of Christ is clearly taught in Scripture. The verses expressly stating this have been quoted in full. These are Matt. 1. 18–20 and Luke 1. 34–35. The Holy Spirit has a *twofold* connection with the Birth of our Lord from the Virgin (Greek, *partheno-genesis*, or Virgin-Birth). (1) In His conception; (2) In securing the sinlessness of His Birth. During the period before birth by His superintendence He kept the Virgin Mary from transmitting to the infant in her womb that taint of original sin which ran as truly in her blood-stream as in any other woman's so that our Lord, alone of all mankind, was born and remained absolutely free from all trace of original sin.

4. THE IMPORTANCE OF JOSEPH

To this great and good and kind man we owe much. "Great calm, great love, great honour, great piety and great strength evidently met in his character" (Richard Glover). He makes three contributions.

(1) **He protects the good name of Mary and of our Lord,** who was commonly accepted as the natural son of Joseph and Mary (Matt. 2. 13–15; 13. 55; Luke 2. 48; John 1. 45).

(2) **He provides for the infant Christ and His mother** through his trade as carpenter (Matt. 13. 55), one which our Lord adopted till He began His public ministry. In Mark 6. 3 He is called "the carpenter". Many infer from this verse that Joseph was at that time dead.

(3) **He transmits to Christ his Crown Rights** (see p. 44). This brings us to the last topic in our study of the Virgin Birth.

5. THE IMPORTANCE OF THE GENEALOGIES

1. THE DIFFERENCE BETWEEN THE GENEALOGIES

There are two genealogies of our Lord, the first contained in Matt. 1. 1–17, and the second in Luke 3. 23–38. These differ in the following respects:

(1) **In Extent:** The genealogy in Matthew goes back as far as Abraham; the one in Luke, however, traces our Lord's ancestry to Adam.

(2) **In Names:** The two genealogies are identical from Abraham to David, but here the lines diverge and, apart from one exception, the names are quite different. Matthew traces the family line of David down through Solomon, and Luke through Solomon's younger brother, Nathan. The exception is in the generation spanned by Salathiel (Shealtiel) and Zerubbabel, in whom the two lines converge and unite, thereafter to separate once more and remain quite apart.

The genealogy in Matthew apparently gives that of Joseph; while that in Luke gives Mary's. In Luke 3. 23 we read, "Jesus himself . . . being [as was supposed] the son of Joseph, which was *the son of* Heli." Whenever in the Authorized Version words occur in italics they are not in the original. The Greek here simply reads "Joseph of Heli". In such a case as this a Greek would supply whatever word the context demanded, it might be son, son-in-law, father, sister, aunt, mother, grandparent. In this case it would be "son-in-law". Heli was Mary's father, and Joseph his son-in-law.

2. THE THREE PROPHECIES AFFECTING THE GENEALOGIES

(1) **The Davidic Covenant Prophecies.** Messianic prophecy had foretold that Christ should come of the seed of David. God had said to him, "I will set up thy seed after thee . . . thine house and thy kingdom shall be established for ever before thee: thy throne shall be established for ever" (2 Sam. 7. 12–16). This prediction looked far beyond Solomon to Christ. Frequently in the Prophets He is said to spring from David (cp. Isa. 11. 1, where David's father, Jesse, is referred to as the root whence the Messiah springs; cp. also Jer. 30. 9 where Christ is actually called "David"; also Ezek. 34. 23–24; 37, 24; Hos. 3. 5). Of David's line undoubtedly the Virgin Mary came (Luke 3. 31).

(2) **The Jehoiachin-Curse Prophecies.** Jehoiachin, the son of Jehoiakim, was the second-last king of the house of David to sit upon the throne. He is also called Jeconiah, and Coniah (cp. 2 Kings

24. 8–16; 2 Chron. 36. 9, 10). In his reign Jeremiah lived and pronounced this malediction upon him, "As I live, saith the Lord, though Coniah the son of Jehoiakim king of Judah were the signet upon my right hand, yet would I pluck thee [Coniah] thence . . . O earth, earth, earth, hear the word of the Lord. Thus saith the Lord, Write ye this man childless, a man that shall not prosper in his days: for no man of his seed shall prosper, sitting upon the throne of David, and ruling any more in Judah" (Jer. 22. 24, 29–30).

(3) **The Zerubbabel-Blessing Prophecy.** Strangely, that very curse using the same figure of a "signet", seems to be lifted in the case of Jehoiachin's descendant, Zerubbabel, who rebuilt the Temple at the command of the prophets, Haggai and Zechariah. Hag. 2. 23 reads, "In that day, saith the Lord of hosts, will I take thee, O Zerubbabel, my servant, the son of Shealtiel [i.e. Salathiel], saith the Lord, and will make thee as a signet: for I have chosen thee, saith the Lord of hosts."

The signet ring on a Persian king's right hand when impressed on the wax seal on a document had the effect of constituting it as law, even as "the law of the Medes and Persians, which altereth not" (see Esther 3. 10–12; 8. 8; also Dan. 6. 8). God hereby gave Zerubbabel power of attorney for Him, as He had once promised the very prophet who had pronounced the earlier curse (see Jer. 15. 19).

3. THE FULFILMENT OF THE THREE PROPHECIES AFFECTING THE GENEALOGIES

These three prophecies, the promise to David, the curse on Jehoiachin and the blessing for Zerubbabel were all fulfilled to the letter.

(1) **The Promise to David** was fulfilled in the following manner. His wife, Queen Bathsheba, had two sons, Solomon and Nathan (2 Sam. 5. 14; 1 Chron. 3. 5). Joseph was descended from Solomon (Matt. 1. 6) but Mary from Nathan (Luke 3. 31). Nevertheless, though she did not come of Solomon's line, she did from David his father's. The angel could truly say, "The Lord God shall give unto him (Jesus Christ) the throne of his *father* David" (Luke 1. 32).

(2) **The Curse upon Jehoiachin** descended in that he was bypassed with Solomon and all the rest of his line, apart from one circumstance, so that we could almost say, not one drop of Jehoiachin's blood (or of Solomon's) flowed in our Saviour's veins.

(3) **The Blessing upon Zerubbabel** fell in that grace took Jehoiachin's descendants, Salathiel and Zerubbabel, and joined their lives in the life-line of the Messiah's ancestry for, as Matt. 1. 12 and Luke 3. 27 show, the lines of Joseph and Mary were converged

and both included these two men. Some drops of their blood did indeed flow in that sacred body of our Lord's. The heaviest curse is sometimes mitigated by later obedience, faith and love as Zerubbabel's story proves.

4. THE CROWN RIGHTS CONFERRED BY THE GENEALOGIES

Our Lord has a double claim to the throne of David—both by Joseph and by Mary.

(1) **Joseph** represented in himself the regal-legal line. Being a direct descendant of David through Solomon he had the crown rights. But for the misfortune of his race he would have been known not as the carpenter of Nazareth but as King Joseph I and, by Jewish law, he could pass on these rights to his foster son, Jesus the Christ.

(2) **Mary** also had throne-rights as a direct descendant of David. By the Daughters-of-Zelophehad Enactment (Num. 27. 1–11; cp. Num. 36) she could receive and transmit to her son her inherited rights. The very fact that she went to be enrolled in Bethlehem, David's old city, as well as Joseph's, confirms what we elsewhere know that she was of royal blood, for had she not had specific claims it would not have been necessary for her (and in her condition) to make the journey. Joseph's presence would have been quite sufficient.

We see then the importance of these genealogies. No orthodox Jew today would for a moment consider the claim of anyone to be the Messiah unless he could show his pedigree through David to Abraham, but these furnish Jesus the Saviour with the needed credentials as the promised King of Israel who, as the direct descendant of David, shall reign for ever from his throne exactly as God has promised.

The very preservation of the documents from which the genealogies were copied by Matthew and Luke shows forth the sovereignty as well as the faithfulness of God. The records were kept in the Temple archives to survive the destruction of God's House at Shiloh (1 Sam. 4. 11 ff.), the overthrow of Solomon's Temple in Jerusalem in 586 B.C., the Invasion of Alexander the Great in 330 B.C. who came within a hairbreadth of destroying the City, and the Civil War terminated by Pompey in 63 B.C. which raged even in the Temple. The precious scrolls continued throughout the dangerous decades of the first century till about A.D. 60 when, apparently, Matthew and Luke were led by God to make transcriptions of the relevant portions of the archives. A few years later the day came, 2nd September, A.D. 70, to be precise, when a Roman soldier, immediately after Titus' taking of Jerusalem, threw a burning torch through a window in the Temple. This lighted on a pile of incense within and set the whole ablaze. In the inferno those archives perished and no imposter could prove his Davidic descent today.

We have covered in this chapter on the Virgin Birth the importance of (1) The Subject; (2) The Mother, Mary; (3) The Holy Spirit; (4) The foster-father, Joseph; (5) The Genealogies. In our next study we examine more minutely the wonder of that which, through the mystery and miracle of the Virgin Birth, came to pass, namely, the Incarnation.

NOTES

NOTES

ADVANCE QUESTIONS ON CHAPTER THREE: THE INCARNATION

1. By "the Incarnation" we mean God the Son becoming Man at the Virgin Birth.

Read carefully the account of the Meat (or Meal) Offering described in Lev. 2. Typically, the fine flour has always been taken to represent the perfect humanity of our Lord, and the olive oil, the Holy Spirit. If this be correct explain in your own words how this offering could aptly symbolize the Incarnation of Christ.

2. In Matt. 3 the Three Persons of the Trinity are all represented as acting separately. What does each do?

3. Give two reasons for Christ's Incarnation from (1) John 1. 14, 18 and (2) Heb. 2.

4. What happened when our Lord ascended? Was it merely His returning to the Father or did it involve something much more? Explain as fully as possible what you think occurred. Acts 2. 33, 36; Phil. 2. 9–11; Heb. 10. 12, 13.

5. Name the classes that are said to be surpassed by Christ in Rom. 8. 38; Eph. 1. 20–22; Phil. 2. 9–11; Col. 1. 16; 2. 15; 1 Pet. 3. 22.

6. Did Christ cease to be a man when He ascended? See Acts 13. 38; 17. 31; 1 Tim. 2. 5; Heb. 2. 6–9; 10. 12; 13. 8.

7. What Psalm is quoted and applied to Christ in Heb. 2. 6–9?

8. In Paul's letters a great deal is said about our identification with Christ. For example in Rom. 6. 3 we are said to be baptized *with Him*. These last two words are repeated in the following passages and indicate various aspects in which this identification applies. Here are the passages: see if you can make a complete chart of the *stages* of identification.

(1) Rom. 6. 8 and Col. 2. 20.
(2) Col. 2. 12.
(3) Rom. 6. 4; Col. 2. 12.
(4) Eph. 2. 6; Col. 2. 12; 3. 1; (see also Rom. 6. 4).
(5) Eph. 2. 6.
(6) Col. 3. 3.

9. (1) In John 1. 18 where is Christ said to dwell?
(2) Where, in Col. 3. 3, are we said to dwell?
(3) Where, therefore, must we also dwell?

10. In what relation are we said to stand to Christ? (1) In Cor. 12. 27; (2) in Eph. 5. 23–32; (3) in Rev. 19. 7–9?

CHAPTER THREE

THE INCARNATION

The Incarnation is the first of the steps in history which God took to bring back mankind to Himself. The others are Christ's Redeeming Death, His Resurrection, His Ascension and Ascension Ministry and the future "fact" of His personal Return. These are the steps that were mentioned in Chapter One.

In Chapter Two the first of these Steps was examined, the Incarnation as an *Event in History*, i.e. The Virgin Birth. The actual people involved were studied—men and women whose footprints are firmly embedded in the sands of time. We thus begin in these studies to look at the Christ we know and love as *The Jesus of History.* That to us He is, and that He will ever remain; as such we are determined never to let Him go!

In this chapter we return to the realm of theology, to study the *significance* for us of the historical fact which we have just surveyed. We aim to see what it means; what it involves; and what is its relation to the other great Steps that God took.

1. THE MEANING OF THE INCARNATION

The term Incarnation comes from two Latin words *in*, "in" and *caro*, "flesh" and means the doctrine that at a given point in time God took upon Himself human flesh and, with it, human nature.

Distinction must be made at once between three ideas which critics think to be separate but which the Evangelical Church in all ages has identified: (1) The Jesus of History otherwise the Man of Galilee, the Prophet of Nazareth, Jesus of Nazareth (see Acts 2. 22; 6. 14 and 22. 8 where Christ Himself assumes it). He is an historical figure and is described in the Gospels and well known to the crowds addressed in Acts. (2) The Christ of Experience, whom the Christians in Acts and today have met, loved and worshipped; and (3) the Christ of the Creeds, such as the Apostles' Creed, or the Nicene Creed. We must continually keep before our eyes the secondary objective of this Series; *to prove that the three are identical.*

The New Testament contends for their identity. For example, the Apostle John was the great exponent of "The Christ of Experience" and wrote his Gospel sixty years after the departure of the Jesus of History. In his Gospel he has his own version of the Virgin Birth:

"The Word (i.e. God the Son) was made flesh, and dwelt among us (literally, lived in a tent among us, i.e. the tent of His human body)" (John 1. 14). This sojourning in a tent covers the thirty-three years of His life on earth. In his First Epistle John stresses this yet again: "Hereby know ye the Spirit of God: Every spirit that confesseth that Jesus Christ *is come in the flesh* is of God: and every spirit that confesseth not that Jesus Christ is come in the flesh is not of God: and this is that spirit of antichrist" (1 John 4. 2, 3).

The Creeds contend for their identity. They stress that He is Very Man of Very Man, no less than that He is Very God of Very God. His true, full and permanent humanity is always a central point. They contend as fiercely for it as for His Deity. For over a century before the heresy of Arianism challenged His divinity, that of Gnosticism attacked His humanity. The Creeds defended one equally with the other.

Scripture, Experience and the Creeds identify as one and the same Person Him whom we variously call "the Jesus of History", "the Christ of Experience" and "the Christ of the Creeds".

2. THE INCARNATION AND THE TRINITY

1. THE NATURE OF THE TRINITY

To understand the meaning of the Incarnation one must first know the meaning of the Trinity, which is this: the Bible teaches the Unity of the Godhead, in opposition to the "gods many and lords many" of the heathen. But it also teaches that this unity is not a simple but a compound one, in that in this same Godhead are Three Persons—the Father, the Son and the Holy Spirit. These sacred Persons are co-equal, co-eternal and consubstantial. Each is possessed of the elements of personality, i.e. thought, feeling, conscience and will, so that there are three separate centres of consciousness, feeling and action within the Trinity. Yet these together constitute one God.

One may think of the Holy Trinity under the figure of an equilateral triangle, a space enclosed by three straight lines of equal length. When these lines are so united as to enclose this space they do not change one iota as to their length or nature, but together they combine to constitute an entity or reality which they never could do if they existed apart. And the entity which they constitute is a unity—it is *one* triangle indivisible and complete, and not three. Just so, the Three Persons of the Godhead, while retaining their separate personalities and relationships one with another and with others human or angelic, form one unitary super-personality, "God in Three Persons, blessed Trinity".

2. PROOFS OF THE TRINITY

The Trinity is a truth superior to our understanding yet not contrary to our reason. It is in Scripture nowhere expressly stated but everywhere implied, as the following proofs show:

(1) **The Three Persons appear together in the Bible.** In Matt. 3. 16, 17 we read that at His Baptism our Lord was standing in the waters of Jordan; the Father was speaking from heaven and the Holy Spirit was descending from the Father to the Son.

(2) **Our relationship to each Person differs**

(*a*) To the *Father* believers are said to be His "sons" or "children" (e.g. John 1. 12, 13). In Scripture they are never spoken of as His "brethren".

(*b*) To the *Son* they stand as "brethren" (Rom. 8. 29; Heb. 2. 11, 12, 17). Corporately, they are said to constitute His "bride" (Eph. 5. 23–32; Rev. 19. 7–9; 21. 2–9; 22. 17). They are not called His "sons".

(*c*) To the *Holy Spirit* believers are never said to stand in the relation of either sons, brothers or bride. He is represented as Christ's Deputy, or Vicegerent, or Representative. He indwells the temple of the believer's body (1 Cor. 6. 19). He builds the composite Temple of Christ formed of living stones (Eph. 2. 20–22). He acts as Comforter or Helper (John 14. 16) but He never appears as Father, as Brother or as Bridegroom. As the relations of the Members of the Trinity with man are distinct, it follows that the Persons themselves must be separate.

(3) **The Three Persons of the Trinity have fellowship with each other.** They address one another; Scripture records many conversations between them (e.g. Psa. 2. 7–9, alluded to by Christ Himself in Rev. 2. 27; Psa. 22. 1; 40. 6–8; cp. Heb. 10. 5–10) Psa. 110. 1; Isa. 49. 3, 5–9; 50. 4–9). Their acts while harmonious and related to a central design, are also quite well defined. The Father sends the Son; the Son sends the Spirit (John 16. 7).

There are many other indications of differentiation of Persons within the Trinity, but the above will indicate the deity of One who became Incarnate.

3. THE INCARNATION AND THE ASCENSION

Both the Incarnation and the Ascension are related to the doctrine of the Trinity. The Ascension is the Incarnation in reverse. The classic definition of both is found in the words of our Lord in John 16. 28, "I came forth from the Father, and am come into the world: again, I leave the world, and go to the Father." In the

Incarnation Christ left the Father and went into the world; in the Ascension He left the world and returned to the Father.

In John's Gospel there are two classes of expression for this Return Journey. (1) Down and Up and (2) From and To. Whichever we read they teach us that the Incarnation meant the Son's leaving heaven personally to come to earth. There was something different about His Incarnation from His pre-Incarnate Theophanies, or "Appearances of Himself as God" in the Old Testament (e.g. Gen. 32. 24–30; Josh. 5. 13–15). During the thirty-three years of His earthly life He was not in heaven but on earth; since His Ascension He is not on earth but with His Father. It is of this longed-for return that He spoke more often in the Gospel of John than of His Resurrection, as the following list shows:

(1) **Down-and-Up Passages** include such as the following: "What and if ye shall see the Son of man *ascend up* where he was before?" (John 6. 62), and "I *came down* from heaven to do the will of him that sent me" (John 6. 38); "The bread of God is he which *cometh down from heaven*" (6. 33). See also John 3. 13; 6. 42, 50, 51, 58.

(2) **From-and-To Passages** are such as these: "I go *unto* the Father" (John 14. 28; cp. 16. 28). "I proceeded forth and *came from* God" (John 8. 42). Note also John's own summary: "Jesus knowing that the Father had given all things into his hands, and that he *was come from God, and went to God*: He riseth from supper" (John 13. 3, 4). See also John 3. 31; 4. 34; 7. 29, 33; 8. 14, 23; 9. 39. To these may be added those passages where the Son speaks of the Father as *sending* Him, for the action of sending (with the thought of returning afterwards) implies a From-and-To Journeying. These are: John 5. 23, 30, 36, 37; 6. 29, 38, 39, 40, 44, 57; 7. 16, 28, 29; 8. 16, 18, 26, 29; 10. 36; 12. 44, 45, 49.

Other references of Christ to His Incarnation and Ascension may be found in John 7. 34; 8. 14, 21, 38 (and cp. 5. 16–30).

The most intimate self-disclosure of all occurs in His prayer to the Father after the Last Supper. He begins by referring to the time He was with the Father before His Incarnation: "And now, O Father, glorify thou me with thine own self with the glory which I had with thee before the world was." He continues, "The men which thou gavest me . . . have known surely that *I came out from Thee* . . . *I come to Thee* . . . Father, I will that they also, whom thou hast given me, be with me where I am; that they may behold my glory, which thou hast given me: for thou lovedst me before the foundation of the world" (John 17. 5, 6, 8, 11, 24).

The first element, therefore, in the Incarnation is that the Son left heaven to come to earth. *The Jesus of History is the Eternal Son who was ever in the bosom of the Father* (John 1. 18).

3. THE INCARNATION AND HUMANITY OF CHRIST

The Incarnation had not only a relation to the Trinity in that Christ left the Father to come to earth, it had also a relation to humanity in that He became for ever a man. He at a moment in time took our human nature into permanent union with His divine nature.

1. THE UNION WAS COMPLETE

The Meal-Offering Illustration.

This union of the two natures is beautifully prefigured in the Meal-Offering of Lev. 2 (miscalled the Meat-Offering), which like the Drink-Offering, was the accompaniment of all the sacrifices. It was like the bread or the glass of water in a restaurant that go with certain meals. You never had the one without the other.

The offering consisted of *fine flour*, representing the perfect humanity of our Lord—not one coarse grain—mingled with *olive oil*, which stands for the Holy Spirit and, hence, for deity. Each became inextricably blended, for ever one. The cake thus compounded was a unit—one cake, not two. After it had been baked it was anointed with the same oil, symbolizing the anointing with the Spirit of the God-Man in the waters of Jordan, as described in Matt. 3. 16, 17.

It should be observed, however, that though the two natures are for ever one they are for ever separate. This distinction will be dealt with in the next chapter. *It is enough here to realize that at the Incarnation the Son became Man.*

2. THE UNION FULFILLED A PURPOSE

The Sunken Tank Illustration.

Sometimes when salvage men wish to raise a sunken wreck they adopt the method followed with the British submarine, *Poseidon*, and sink alongside it great tanks. These are lashed to the wreck then emptied of water and filled with air to render them buoyant. They rise, but because they are fastened so as to have become part of the wreck, they float it along with themselves. When God wished to raise the sunken wreck of our humanity He did not drop His Word like a rescript on parchment and float it down over the battlements of heaven. "The Word became flesh" (John 1. 14 R. V.). He became a baby. He became in Christ what we are, that we might become what He is. *He became Man that we might be raised to the central height of Godhead.*

3. THE UNION WAS PERMANENT

The Chinese Missionary Illustration.

The Manhood of our Lord was not something that He laid aside when, at His Ascension, He returned to heaven for He took it with Him. He has never ceased to be Man; He never will. That is why it is not strictly true to say that the Ascension is merely the Incarnation in reverse, it involves much more.

In the old days when missionaries went to China they used to speak Chinese, think in Chinese, and often wear Chinese clothes and almost look like the Chinese. When however they came home they left all that behind. When Christ became Man it was Man for ever that He remained. There is a *man* in the glory. We can therefore say,

O my Lord, I love Thee, worship and adore;
God from everlasting, Man for evermore.

We must never forget that it was a *man* that was born; a *man* that died; a *man* that rose; a *man* that ascended; a *man* that pleads in the glory; and a *man* that is coming again to judge the world.

Paul said, "There is one God, and one mediator between God and men, the *man* Christ Jesus" (1 Tim. 2. 5). On Mars Hill in Athens he said that God "hath appointed a day, in the which he will judge the world in righteousness by that *man* whom he hath ordained; whereof he hath given assurance unto all men, in that he hath raised him from the dead" (Acts 17. 31; see also 13. 38; Heb. 2. 5–9; 10. 12–20; Rev. 5. 6, etc.). *The human Jesus of History remains centrally embedded in the New Testament doctrine of the Divine Christ.*

4. THE INCARNATION AND THE SUBSTITUTIONARY DEATH OF CHRIST

The Incarnation was an essential step to be taken to secure the redemption of mankind. This was for two reasons; first, to be able to die; second, to be able to represent mankind.

1. CHRIST WAS BORN TO DIE

Redemption involves a vicarious death—someone dying in place of the guilty one. God cannot die; man can, and only if the Son became man could He die. He was literally "born to die". Heb. 2. 9 says so. "Jesus . . . was made a little lower than the angels *for the suffering of death* . . . that He by the grace of God should taste death for every man."

In passing, note that there was something in Christ's death that will never be in ours as Christians. At that hour the Christian may think himself forsaken but God will be there; He has promised never to leave nor to forsake us. But when Christ died, He was made sin for us who knew no sin, and the Father's presence had to be withdrawn. This separation from God is the real penalty of sin (Matt. 27. 46; 2 Cor. 5. 21).

2. CHRIST WAS BORN TO REPRESENT MANKIND

God cannot represent man in sacrifice. Only man can do that. Christ became man that He might on behalf of all mankind offer His life. Note how in Rom. 5. 12–21 where Paul, stressing the representative character of Adam's and of Christ's acts says, "By one man (Adam) sin entered into the world, and death by sin; and so death passed upon all men, for that all have sinned . . . But not as the offence, so also is the free gift. For if through the offence of one many be dead, much more the grace of God, and the gift by grace, which is by one *man, Jesus Christ*, hath abounded unto many." This matter is dealt with again, more fully, in Chapter Seven.

3. CHRIST'S REDEMPTION IS FOR ALL MEN

Christ's Redemption is made for all mankind—all that ever have lived; all that ever will and not for the "elect" only. Scripture is perfectly plain on this subject, and leaves us no alternative position (otherwise words have no meaning).

John the Baptist, whom the Lord called "a burning and a shining light" and said that he spoke "the truth" (John 5. 33, 35) said of Christ, "Behold the Lamb of God, which taketh away the sin of *the world*" (John 1. 29). "The world" in Scripture, especially in John's writing, means the whole mass of mankind, loved by God (John 3. 16) and savable, but at present under the domination of Satan who is its "prince" (John 14. 30) and its "god" (2 Cor. 4. 4). Christ, as a sacrificial Lamb, died for the sin of *all men* and in their place. In 1 John 2. 2 the Apostle says that "Jesus Christ . . . is the propitiation for our sins, and not for our's only, but also for the sins of *the whole world*." "Propitiation" here means the sacrifice which makes it morally possible for God to unlock the storehouse of His love for us, and to bless us with a blessing that no angel has ever experienced.

Paul in 2 Cor. 5. 14, 15 says that Christ "died for all" and in 1 Tim. 2. 4 he writes "God our Saviour, who will [Greek, *thelō*] have all men to be saved, and to come unto the knowledge of the truth" and adds that Christ "gave himself a ransom [Greek, *antilutron*] for *all*" (v. 6).

The word *anti*, in Greek, always implies substitution. Something is taken away, and something else is substituted for it. *Lutron* means a ransom, literally that which releases. Our lives were forfeited, and Christ's unforfeited life was substituted for ours as a ransom, even "for all".

Peter, in 2 Pet. 3. 9, has a parallel word. He says that "The Lord is . . . not willing [Greek, *boulomai*] that any should perish, but that all should come to repentance." In Classical Greek *thelō* tends to mean, "to will", and *boulomai* merely "to wish", though some scholars say that in Hellenistic Greek in the first century, the meanings were reversed. One rather doubts this (cp. use in Philem. 13, 14) but the important thing is that, whichever view one takes about the force of *thelō* or *boulomai*, both words were used in the above passages.

In Matt. 18. 14 our Lord says, "It is not the will [*thelēma*] of your Father which is in heaven, that one of these little ones should perish." All children that grow up become men or women; obviously it is God's will that they should be saved. Compare Ezek. 18. 31–32; 33. 11 where God says that "I have no pleasure in the death of the wicked".

Our Lord in Luke 22. 37 applied to Himself the Servant-Prophecy of Isa. 53. The verse He referred to was v. 12 but, as the prophecy is one, He in fact maintained that vv. 4–6 describe His substitutionary sufferings. These state that He died for all: "He was wounded for our transgressions, he was bruised for our iniquities: the chastisement of our peace was upon him; and with his stripes we are healed. All we like sheep have gone astray . . . and the Lord hath laid on him the iniquity of us all."

In Heb. 2. 9 it is written that the purpose of Christ's Incarnation was "that *he by the grace of God should taste death for every man*".

4. CHRIST'S UNIVERSAL REDEMPTION IS NOT UNIVERSAL SALVATION (UNIVERSALISM)

The Bible says, "Return unto me; for I have redeemed thee" (Isa. 44. 22). One may be redeemed, but if the conditions of repentance and faith are not fulfilled, if the offer is not closed with, the redemption is without effect. Thus a cancer remedy might be discovered and offered free to all, but not all would thereby be saved. Some would never hear, some would hear and not believe, some would hear and believe but not actually take the remedy; all would die. Only those who, hearing, believed and by an *act* of faith actually took the remedy, would live. (Jas. 2. 14–26 defines faith as more than an intellectual assent; it is a belief which *acts*. His illustrations of Abraham and Rahab make this clear.)

Christ's Incarnation (the Jesus of History) was planned by God so that He should represent humanity and by dying offer His infinite life as a redemption for all mankind.

5. THE INCARNATION AND THE RESURRECTION OF CHRIST

The Incarnation is implied in the Resurrection of Christ, otherwise His Resurrection would not have its present meaning. It was not merely the God-Man that arose from the dead, but God remaining Man, i.e. with His *human* body.

Three facts are true of the Resurrection Body of our Lord. First, it was a *real* body that rose out of the tomb; second it was a *metamorphosed* or transformed body; and third, it was an *identical* body. These facts have a relation to the Ascension.

1. IT WAS A REAL BODY THAT ROSE FROM THE TOMB

It was no phantom. The messianic Psa. 16 says in vv. 9 and 10, "My *flesh* also shall rest in hope . . . for Thou wilt not suffer thine Holy One to see corruption", cp. Acts 2. 25–31; 13. 34–37. A human body was laid in Joseph's tomb and a human body came out of it. With that same human body Christ ate "a piece of broiled fish, and of an honeycomb" (Luke 24. 42) and said, "Handle me and see; for a spirit hath not *flesh and bones*, as ye see me have" (Luke 24. 39), and He spoke to Thomas to, "Reach hither thy finger, and behold my hands; and reach hither thy hand, and thrust it into my side" (John 20. 27). (Note: When Christ, in John 20. 17, said to Mary, "Touch me not," the Greek word used, *haptomai*, should be translated "detain." It means "fasten upon" and gives a life-like picture of Mary clinging to her risen Lord, and refusing to let Him go.)

2. IT WAS A METAMORPHOSED BODY THAT ROSE FROM THE TOMB

The term metamorphosis comes from the Greek word, *morphē* (pron. morfay, translated "form" and meaning, (*a*) the innermost essence of a thing plus, (*b*) its outward appearance). A good example of such a change is that of the metamorphosis of the caterpillar into a butterfly. "Meta" in composition here has the force of the Latin *trans* (as in "*trans*formed") and means the exchanging of one *morphē*, form, for another.

Our Lord's body had various metamorphoses, or form changes.

One was on the Mount of Transfiguration when we read that He was "transfigured" or metamorphosed (Greek, *meta-morpho-o*) before Peter, James and John (Matt. 17. 2). The second was at His Resurrection, when this body could rise through the graveclothes that were about His body and His head, leaving them an empty cast (John 20. 6–8) and could pass through a heavy, locked door (John 20. 19). With this resurrection body our Lord was said to walk twelve miles "in another form" (*morphē*, Mark 16. 12) with two of His disciples, Cleophas and a friend, without being at once recognized (Luke 24. 13–35). In this form, which was now familiar to John, He ascended.

Apparently at His Ascension He would receive the glory of form that was His before His Incarnation, something infinitely more wonderful than anything John or Peter saw. John says, "It doth not yet appear what we shall be: but we know that, when he shall appear, we shall be like him; for we shall see him as he is" (1 John 3.2). This implies that John had not seen Him even after resurrection as He really is. Christ refers to this former glory that was yet to be given to His very body in His prayer in John 17. 5, "Father, glorify thou me with thine own self with the glory which I had with thee before the world was."

3. IT WAS AN IDENTICAL BODY THAT ROSE FROM THE TOMB

This is clear from the fact that Mary recognized Him by the timbre of His voice, as He spoke one word—her name—(John 20. 16) that the Emmaus' disciples could declare, "how that he was made known of them in breaking of bread" (Luke 24. 35) in which two facts apparently revealed Him. First, the nailprints identified Him as He revealed those scarred hands in the act of breaking the stiff, pancake-like loaves and, second, by the characteristic word, "Father", which in Aramaic is "Abba". This word later passed with three other Aramaic words—Amen, Hallelujah and Maranatha (1 Cor. 16. 22)—into the vocabulary even of non-Jewish Christians the world over (cp. Rom. 8. 15; Gal. 4. 6). The circumstances when Thomas thrust finger and hand into nail-prints and spear wound is a further mark of an identity later to be carried to the skies. Here it reappears in glory in the symbolic language of Rev. 5. 6 where John exclaims, "I beheld, and, lo, in the midst of the throne and of the four beasts, and in the midst of the elders, stood a Lamb [Greek, *arnion*] *as it had been slain*." Once again the Jesus of History re-emerges as the Christ of Pentecost, of the Damascus road, of the primitive Church's baptismal formulae. He is still the Christ of Experience, for the Evangelist does not now call Him in the Greek *amnos*, i.e. Lamb, the sole word he uses in his Gospel, but a diminutive expressing extreme, tender and reverent love, *arnion*. literally, "the little lamb". Diminutives in Greek, as in English, are used to express affection and so—the dear Lamb—would perhaps most nearly translate it if only one could utter it with the affectionate awe of Samuel Rutherford.

The Incarnation preconditions the Resurrection of our Lord whose body, the human body of the Jesus of History, real and identical although glorified, rose from the tomb.

6. THE INCARNATION AND THE ASCENSION OF CHRIST

The Ascension of Christ was a divine act occurring like the Virgin Birth, the Substitutionary Death and the Resurrection, at a given point in time, apparently forty days after the Resurrection (Acts 1. 3) though some (despite John 20. 17) prefer to place it immediately after that event. It is as strategically important as the other events and involves at least five factors:

1. THE ASCENSION MEANS THE RETURN OF THE SON TO THE IMMEDIATE PRESENCE OF THE FATHER AND THE SPIRIT

This was discussed earlier in this chapter.

2. THE ASCENSION MEANS THE RESUMPTION BY THE SON OF THE USE OF ALL THE DIVINE ATTRIBUTES AND PREROGATIVES

His Incarnation involved the temporary laying aside of the use of some, though not the possession of any of these (cp. John. 17. 5; Phil. 2. 6–8; Heb. 2. 5–10). See Chapter Five.

3. THE ASCENSION MEANS THE RECEIVING BY THE SON FROM THE FATHER, GLORY, HONOUR AND REWARD FOR THE HUMILIATION OF THE CROSS

Several passages make this glory something far more than even that glory that was His before. They link the "sufferings of Christ" with "the glory that should follow" (1 Pet. 1. 11; Phil. 2. 6–11; Heb. 2. 9; cp. Acts 2. 33–36). This involved receiving power and authority far greater than that of any angel, satanic or divine. Christ hence said, "All power [Greek *exousia*, authority] is given unto me in heaven and in earth" (Matt. 28. 18). It is *because* He became man that He is now thus exalted.

The "newness" of this glory is also suggested by His saying to the Church in Philadelphia in Rev. 3. 12, "I will write upon him my *new* name." In Scripture a change of name usually signifies a new status or office (e.g. Gen. 17. 5, 15; 32. 27, 28; Hos. 1. 6, 9; 2. 1, a change mentioned by Peter in 1 Pet. 2. 10).

The Empire State Building Illustration

First here is a description of this wonder of the modern world. It is a skyscraper built on two acres of ground in New York in 1937. It has 102 storeys above street level (and a lot more below it) and stands 1,248 feet high. Five hundred times it has been struck by lightning, but without harm, for its great steel frame acts as a lightning conductor and protects all other buildings within a mile radius. It never sways even in the highest wind. So strong is that frame that when a few years ago a B-25 bomber hit the 78th floor, one engine going clear through the building, a messenger boy absorbed in a comic on the 85th floor knew nothing about it and calmly went on reading! Through the structure run 3,200 miles of telegraph and telephone wires and 50 miles of plumbing pipes. As to steps—if you want to walk from bottom to top you can, but you must climb 1,860 of them! Most people, however, take one or other of the 72 lifts which go up and down in their seven miles of shafting.

It is from these lifts, particularly the express lifts, that an illustration may be drawn. The first stop is not so far from the top and it takes three minutes to get there. Imagine one of these lifts starting some floors below street level, then halting at ground floor. If our Lord merely rose from the dead that is just what it would be—stopping at ground level. A Man has died, and a Man rises. But watch this lift. Up, up, up . . . and still up, up, up, up it goes—on up past doctors' offices, syndicate offices, up, up, up, ever up—past every imaginable dignitary, civic and state—on up, up till it reaches the very top. "That," says Paul, "is what happened to my Saviour, Jesus. Oh, that you Ephesians might know that same mighty power that was working in Him (and is actually working in you) when God the Father not only raised Him from the dead, but brought Him at the Ascension back to His own dear right side, far above all principality and power, and every name and throne and dominion that is named—all the good angels and archangels—Michael left behind like a mere child, Gabriel that stands in God's presence, abandoned far in the rear—all the bad angels long before hopelessly outclassed—on up, up, still up He goes right to the very throne of God. (See Eph. 1. 19–21.)

4. THE ASCENSION MEANS THE INCORPORATING BY CHRIST OF OUR HUMANITY IN THE CENTRAL HEIGHT OF THE GODHEAD

The Wooden Triangle Illustration.

(1) **The Pre-Existence of the Son in the Trinity.** The Incarnation in relation to the Trinity may be likened to an equilateral wooden triangle made of mahogany. Though subsisting as one triangle it is comprised of three isosceles triangles, each exactly equal and fitting perfectly together. Mahogany in our illustration represents the divine nature. The three triangles stand for the three Persons of the Trinity, for ever co-existing, consubstantial, coeternal. Let this rest on a table, standing for heaven.

(2) **The Incarnation.** One of these triangles, representing the Son, is placed upon the floor which stands for this world. It is still mahogany. This illustrates the Incarnation. When Christ came to earth He left the Father, but retained wholly His divine nature even while on earth.

At the moment of the Second Triangle being placed on the floor imagine that there is tenoned into it a shaft of oak. Let oak stand for humanity. This represents what took place, as already explained, at the Virgin Birth. The Incarnation involved Christ taking into everlasting association our human nature with His divine nature. He united from now on two natures in one person.

(3) **The Ascension.** Let the second triangle now be restored to its position on the table. This represents what took place at our Lord's Ascension. It was not merely His going back where He was before; this would occasion the angels no surprise. It was His taking back there *our humanity.* What a stir there was among them at this event! (For their position cp. 1 Pet. 1. 12; 3. 22; Heb. 1. 6–9, 13, 14; 2. 5.)

This wonderful fact Caroline Noel has beautifully expressed in her great hymn, "In the Name of Jesus", of which two of the verses read,

Humbled for a season, to receive a name
From the lips of sinners unto whom He came,
Faithfully He bore it spotless to the last,
Brought it back victorious when from death He passed.

Bore it up triumphant with its human light,
Through all ranks of creatures to the central height;
To the Throne of Godhead, to the Father's breast,
Filled it with the glory of that perfect rest.

(4) **The Church.** But this is not all. Once more place the triangle on the floor and into the oak (the human nature of Christ)

imagine to be tenoned another piece of oak (the human nature of Christians, i.e. the Church). When that "Second Triangle" resumed its former position, i.e. when the Son ascended "up where he was before" (John 6. 62), He did not merely take His human nature to the skies, *He took ours as well.*

The oak of our humanity is for ever tenoned into the oak of Christ's humanity and both are hidden, recessed as it were, for ever in the mahogany of Godhead. Peter says that Christians are made partakers of the divine nature (2 Pet. 1. 1–4) and Christ implied this oneness when He said, "I am the vine, ye are the branches" (John 15. 5). It is a life-union.

It is a *Man* that is in the glory. But this Man stands to us in the relation of Head to Body, and Bridegroom to Bride. You cannot have the Head with one status and the Body with another; you cannot have the Bridegroom at the head of the table and the Bride sitting with the servants at the foot. Paul made it clear that as Christ was identified with us in our humiliation, so we are with Him in all the steps leading to His exaltation. Thus we are said to be: (*a*) *baptized with Him* unto death (Rom. 6. 3); (*b*) and hence *dead with Him* (Rom. 6. 8; Col. 2. 20); (*c*) *buried with Him* (Rom. 6. 4; Col. 2. 12); (*d*) *risen with Him* (Col. 2. 12; 3. 1; Eph. 2. 6); (*e*) *seated with Him* in the heavenly places far above all principality and power (Eph. 2. 6), and finally, (*f*) *hid with Him* (Col. 3. 3).

The Christian on earth is thus in the safest place in the universe. The late Dr. Donald Grey Barnhouse of Philadelphia used to illustrate it thus: he took a card, held it up and said, "This is the believer." He took his Bible, held it up and said, "This is Christ." He touched his jacket and said, "Let this represent the Father." Then he preached a sermon without saying a word. He first put the card in the Bible and then he tucked the Bible under his jacket.

Being *seated* with Christ ensures fellowship and authority; being *hidden* with Christ ensures fellowship and safety.

5. THE ASCENSION MEANS THAT CHRIST IS STRATEGICALLY PLACED TO AID HIS CHURCH ON EARTH

The character of Christ's present ministry in the glory must be fully realized. When He was on earth He worked; now the Holy Spirit is on earth, He also works; and now that Christ is in the glory He, too, is working.

It is quite true that in two respects He is said to be seated now in the heavenly places. (1) With regard to offering no more sacrifice for sins, His sacrifice is complete and never to be repeated (Heb. 10. 12). (2) With regard to gaining a decisive victory over the devil: this, too, is won and from henceforth He is seated (Psa.

110. 1). He has exchanged His State of Humiliation for that of Exaltation but not yet the Cross for the Sword. He is still the Saviour, not the Judge. Hence He said to persecuting Paul, "Saul, Saul, why persecutest thou me?" (Acts 9. 4). He is the Head while the Church is the body, and there cannot be the body on earth writhing in agony and the Head in heaven in untroubled calm. Christ does *sit*, as far as redemption and victory over Satan are concerned, yet when His Stephen was about to ascend to Him by way of a martyr's death He *stood* to receive Him. Hence Stephen said, "I see the heavens opened, and the Son of man *standing* on the right hand of God" (Acts 7. 56). If the finger is pricked the first to feel it is the head, not the finger, for truly,

There is no place where earth's sorrows
Are more felt than up in heaven.

Well also does Michael Bruce express this truth in his great hymn:

Where high the heavenly Temple stands, the house of God not made with hands,
A Great High Priest our nature wears, the Guardian of Mankind appears.

He who for men their surety stood, and poured on earth His precious blood,
Pursues in heaven His mighty plan, the Saviour and the Friend of man.

Though now ascended up on high, He bends on earth a brother's eye,
Partaker of the human name, He knows the frailty of our frame.

Our fellow-sufferer yet retains a fellow-feeling for our pains,
And still remembers in the skies His tears, His agonies and cries.

In every pang that rends the heart, the Man of Sorrows had a part;
He sympathizes with our grief, and to the sufferer sends relief.

This ministry would, as taught in Hebrews, have been impossible but for His Incarnation, "In all things it behoved him to be made like unto his brethren, that he might be a merciful and faithful high priest in things pertaining to God . . . *For in that he himself hath suffered being tempted*, he is able to succour them that are tempted" (2. 17, 18). "We have not an high priest which cannot be touched with the feeling of our infirmities; *but was in all points tempted like as we are*, yet without sin" (4. 15; cp. 5. 1, 2).

The fact that it is a *Man* that is ascended gives every son of man a way of access by Him to the Father. Christ says, "I am the way, the truth, and the life; no man cometh unto the Father, *but by me*" (John 14. 6), and Heb. 10. 19–22 affirms that men may have "boldness to enter into the holiest by the blood of Jesus, by a new and living way, which he hath consecrated for us, through the veil, that is to say, his *flesh*." Again, it is a *Man* in the glory; for the veil in part typified His flesh in that it was rent (Matt. 27. 51) yet, because of the Resurrection, He is yet a "*living* way". Christ said the same, when He promised, "Him that cometh to me I will in no wise cast out" (John 6. 37).

The Telephone Illustration.

In the early days of telephones when direct dialling was impossible, if a young man in Birmingham wished to contact his father in Edinburgh it was of no use to try to dial his number, as say WAVerley 3344. He simply dialled "O" (for operator) who got his call through and kept him in touch; soon he was speaking with his father.

Just so, whoever and whatever you are, if you wish to get into touch with the God who created the telescope stars and the yet more distant radio stars, you will search in vain in the Bodleian and Cambridge Libraries, the library of the British Museum or the Welsh National Library at Aberystwyth for a formula. But the Bible supplies the formula. There is no need to have a university degree to master it. It consists of just one word, the precious name "Jesus". Call on that name and instantly He is with you. Do not try to contact the Father direct—call upon Jesus. After you have been talking with Him for a little while you will find the Father at His elbow. "He that hath the Son hath the Father also" (2 John 9). Communion with the Father can be obtained and maintained only by proceeding with relations with the Son. Then all is so natural, so easy. By-pass your Mediator and you get nowhere; you lose the presence of God. Keep abiding in Christ and you dwell automatically in the bosom of the Father.

The Ascension means that the Jesus of History, who is also the Eternal Son, returned to the immediate presence of the Father, not only resuming the use of His divine prerogatives but also receiving from the Father a new glory and dominion at the same time incorporating our humanity in the central height of Godhead, thence as our High Priest to carry on His work of aiding mankind.

SUMMARY

On the precious historic fact of the Incarnation all the other work of God relative to our salvation depends. The Atonement, the Resurrection, Pentecost, the Second Coming, would all be impossible but for the prior fact that "God became Man".

Here are the central doctrinal truths that have been touched on:

1. The Trinity consists of Three Persons in one Godhead, with three separate personalities, but a single nature.

2. God the Son took human nature into permanent and indivisible association with His eternal divine nature at His Virgin Birth.
3. God the Son at His Ascension took this newly appropriated human nature to the central height of Godhead where He was before the Incarnation.
4. The effect of His Incarnation, with the following Death, Resurrection and Ascension, is to raise the sunken wreck of humanity to the central height of Godhead along with Himself.
5. The remote and unknown God is now intimately accessible at once to every man calling upon the name of the God-Man, Christ Jesus.

NOTES

NOTES

NOTES

ADVANCE QUESTIONS ON CHAPTER FOUR

1. Some people say that it does not matter what you believe in Religion, as long as you are *sincere*. Is this correct? Demonstrate your answer (1) from experience in other walks of life (2) from Scripture.

2. "Is it necessary to have a Creed? If people have a simple experience of God working in their lives, is not that enough?" What do *you* think about this? Why?

3. "Perhaps it is all right to have a simple basic creed, like the Apostles' Creed, or the Doctrinal Basis of the Inter-Varsity Fellowship, but why go in for creeds that are elaborate and are sometimes hard to understand?" Give reasons for your answer.

4. How would you define the word, "Personality"? What are the elements that constitute it?

5. What attributes (or characteristics) does God have that we do not have? In what ways is He different from man?

6. In Gen. 1. 27 we are told that God made man "in his own image". In what respects is this true?

7. Would you say that sinfulness is an *essential* part of human nature? The word "essential" is used to mean that without which the true nature of a thing would not be the same. Prove what you say.

8. Christians often say that Christ had two natures, a divine and a human one. Does this mean that He had also two personalities?

9. Work through the following Scriptures and you will find some apparent contradictions between Christ's ability as God and His limitations as man. Define the limitations in the first group of Scriptures and compare them with the statements made about God in the second:

(1) Mark 4. 38; Luke 22. 43, 44; John 4. 6 as opposed to Isa. 40. 28.
(2) Matt. 4. 2; John 19. 28 as opposed to Psa. 50. 12.
(3) Matt. 24. 36; Mark 6. 38; Mark 11. 13 as opposed to Psa. 139. 1–4; Isa. 40. 28; Heb. 4. 13.
(4) Psa. 2. 7; Luke 2. 7; Acts 13. 33 as opposed to Psa. 90. 2; Isa. 57. 15, yet cp. Mic. 5. 2; Heb. 7. 3.
(5) Luke 2. 52 as opposed to Psa. 102. 26, 27 yet cp. Heb. 1. 10–12.

10. What attribute of deity mentioned in Psa. 139. 7–12 is claimed by Christ in Matt. 18. 20; 28. 19–20?

11. What is the difference between "ubiquity" and "omnipresence"?

12. Is the devil omnipresent? Prove your answer.

13. Can you find any instances where:

(1) Christ worshipped the Father as God?
(2) Christ was worshipped by men as God?

14. Christ is said in the creeds to be equal with the Father in power and glory. How could you reconcile this with 1 Cor. 15. 28?

15. Which is true to say that Christ is "of exactly the same nature as the Father" or "of very similar nature to the Father"? How can you prove this from Scripture?

CHAPTER FOUR

THE UNION OF THE TWO NATURES

IN the previous chapter a series of pictures was presented illustrating what the Incarnation means to men *in experience.* The historic facts of the life of Jesus—His pre-existent life with the Father, His Birth, His Death, His Resurrection, His Ascension, His Ministry in the Skies—were in that chapter related to the facts that affect personal everyday experience as Christians.

Man could not know communion with the risen Christ as one who is both man and God but for His Virgin Birth and Resurrection; nor forgiveness but for the Cross; nor victory over the powers of hell but for the Ascension. The Jesus of History is essential to the Christ of Experience, as one side of a coin is to the existence of the other.

In this study one step further is taken—past the Jesus of History and the Christ of Experience to the Christ of the Creeds. If this last can be proved as identical with the other two the underlying purpose of this series is fulfilled. In this chapter it is not possible to prove this identity, but the student can establish what is to be proved, for it describes how the Creeds—and in particular the Nicene—define Jesus Christ. The proof follows in later volumes.

In this undertaking the student will become possessed of various important tools—one might almost call them "Friends"—which will later help greatly in evaluating the Jesus of History and the Christ of the Creeds. These are "Ideas", or "Concepts", and it is essential that the new student of theology should have a thorough grasp of them from the very first, for they form its alphabet.

At this stage it is confined to one narrow aspect of theology only—that is, the *Manner* in which the Lord's two natures, the human and the divine, were united in the One Person. The theological name for this is the "Hypostatic Union", from a Greek word, *hypostasis,* which was used with a good deal of confusion and looseness in the early church, sometimes (as here) meaning substance or nature, but later referring to person, or personality.

To anyone who is not used to dealing with abstract thoughts and ideas, this subject can be very difficult, yet it is vital for the student to grasp it thoroughly. An endeavour has been made to make it both clear and interesting. The most important thing is to separate the ideas and to master them one at a time.

The Council at Nicea

In June of the year 325 occurred the first meeting of the world-wide church at Nicea. Constantine summoned it, giving the delegates free passes on the great Imperial Posting Roads. Thus some by highway, others by sea, appeared. Men who were only names—heroes of arena and dungeon that one never expected to see in this world, were there. There were over forty bishops from Syria and Palestine; another eighty from the Roman province of Asia Minor; twenty more came scudding along in a lumbering Alexandrian corn-ship driven before the southern trade-wind, among them Athanasius, the great champion of orthodoxy of all ages, fine of feature, clear of mind, mighty in knowledge, holy in life and Greek in nationality (of whom more later). Twelve more came from the Balkans; others included veteran missionaries to the Goths, and old Nicholas of Myra (Acts 27. 5), and the original Santa Claus! Emissaries, too, there were, from North Africa, from Rome and Spain. All met in Nicea, the famous holiday resort on the shores of the Black Sea, the watering place of the Empire. What a collection they turned out to be! One minus an eye, another with only one leg, yet another twisted half double with tortures of rack and brand, a fourth with flesh seamed by the lash—all the victorious survivors of the last of a series of ten terrible persecutions, whose ashes were barely cold. Constantine's "conversion" in the year 313 had ended all that and now he himself summoned the Council, paid for the expenses, and organized a first class final banquet (not one absentee for that) at the close!

The main reason for their turning up from all parts of the Empire (at the command of the good Emperor) was to sort out what the Bible really does teach, and the Church really is to believe, about the Person of Christ, and the way His two natures fit in together.

At first thought an onlooker might fairly ask, "Well, what does it matter anyway? The main thing is the Apostles' Creed, which states, as we have seen, that 'Christ was conceived by the Holy Ghost, born of the Virgin Mary' ". It would be convenient to have a loose, general, elastic sort of creed—all right, until someone starts to preach something quite wrong, which yet comes within the terms of this same loose, flexible, general, happy-go-lucky document. It does not violate anything in it, and yet it is wrong—violently and blasphemously and dangerously wrong. What can be done? The only possible thing is to ascertain what is surely believed; to cut out loose, vague terms and expressions that look two ways and might be construed to mean two different things; to get down to brass tacks, and think far more accurately and clearly than ever had been thought before—to decide what is meant, and what is not, then to state it. This is the only way to trap a "waterman theologian", a man looking one way and rowing another.

The waterman, by the way, who sparked all this off was a presbyter born in or near Alexandria whose name was Arius. He was an early modernist. He lived not too good a life but was a very clever fellow, and very ingenious at propaganda and at turning the tables on all his opponents and in causing divisions which he used in his own favour. His doctrine, which is called Arianism, was that Christ was not really one with the Father at all, but was created by Him in time, and He in turn created the world. So He was merely the first of all created beings. He was divine—oh, yes, but only in the sense that all men have the divine spark, only in His case He had a much bigger spark. He is finite. Arius said, "even if He is called God He is not God truly, but by participation in grace. . . . He too is called God in name only." He had a substance or nature *similar* to the Father, but not *the same as* He had. "God" was a courtesy title for Christ. He was not and is not God but a demigod. Only God's power kept Him from sinning. This was what Arius believed, but he was such a master of finesse and double meaning it was very difficult to corner him. He had found breaches in the current simple creeds of the Church big enough to drive a chariot through at a gallop. This plausible trickster was as slippery as an eel. There was, therefore, only one thing to be done; to erect a sieve with mesh fine enough to keep reptiles of his sort out. This sieve is now called the Nicene Creed.

Who the chief actors were in this ecclesiastical drama, what they said and did and how it all turned out in the end (after somersaulting many times before and after Nicea) would form another day's story. The theological concern at this elementary stage is merely to grip the chief concepts, thoughts, ideas, principles, doctrines or fragments of doctrines about Christ that in those days were flying about thick as snow in an Alpine storm, and reduce them to twentieth-century English. The various technical terms employed at Nicea and in textbooks today are given with explanations to label these thoughts.

This Study consists of a procession of ideas which is like the introduction of guests at some reception. These assemble outside the door to the Great Hall, just inside of which the reader, like host and hostess stand, and it is the work of the writer, like some old bent servant of the place, to have them approach the host one at a time, to announce the name of each one, giving the briefest introduction about him. After this he must stand alongside the other guests within the room. Only enough will be said to help the reader form a nodding acquaintance with them now in readiness for later occasions. For some nervous hosts it is always a certain trial and embarrassment to have introduced to them more and yet more people—but cheer up—though there are many of them this time, and some very big personalities among them, it will soon be over. So brace yourself to receive

GUEST NO. 1: THE IDEA OF PERSONALITY

Personality is the possession of four component parts—thought, feeling, will and conscience. If anybody lacked one of these he would not be a person. To be without thought would mean being an imbecile; without feeling, a robot; without will, a jelly-fish; and without conscience, a monster. A person is someone with these four essentials. God is a Person and when the Bible says that He made man in His own image (Gen. 1. 27), it means He made humanity with these four same essentials that constitute His own personality, thus making men in a limited degree capable of fellowship with Him. Augustine once said, "Thou hast made us for Thyself and our hearts are restless until they find their rest in Thee." How true this is!

As there are Three Persons in the Godhead it means that there are three separate centres of consciousness each with separate feeling, thought, will and conscience, yet so attuned that they think, feel and will as one.

The word "person" comes from two Latin words *per*, "through", and *sono*, "to sound", and originally was used of an actor's mask, for it was through this that he spoke on the stage. Thence it came to mean the character impersonated by the actor, which explains our use of the term "Dramatis Personae". Thirdly it was used of the actor who thus represented a character. Lastly it assumed today's meaning of "person".

The Greek equivalent of *persona* is *hypostasis* but, as already said, it previously was so loosely used that while sometimes it meant "person" at other times it had been used to mean "nature", which is something quite different.

At this levée, the first Guest having been introduced, the second now takes his place for announcement as

GUEST NO. 2: THE IDEA OF NATURE

Men *are* persons; they *have* a nature, though nature itself is impersonal. Our nature is called human nature. It is common to every man, woman and child that has ever lived in this world. There are other natures in existence today as well as human—angelic nature, demonic nature, animal nature and divine nature. Men are persons with a human nature; God the Father, God the Son and God the Spirit are Persons with a divine nature. They always had this; they always will.

The characteristics of the divine nature are at least ten: they are 1. Omniscience (knowing everything); 2. Omnipresence (being everywhere); 3. Omnipotence (being all powerful); 4. Transcendence (being apart from the universe, i.e. everything else that exists, and infinitely superior to it); 5. Unchangeability (or Immutability); 6. Self-existence (or Immortality); 7. Infinity; and then follow the three great moral attributes—8. infinite and absolute Holiness; 9. Wisdom; and 10. Love. These make God to be God.

There are nine synonyms that theologians use for nature. These are in three languages, English, Latin and Greek, but must be known. Here they are. All mean exactly the same thing.

Nature: the Latin is *natura*, and the Greek, *phusis*.

Essence: the Latin is *essentia*, and the Greek, *ousia*. (The Latin "to be" is *esse*, so *essentia* is simply *being*. The Greek *ousia* likewise is the noun formed from the feminine particle of the Greek word "to be".)

Substance: the Latin is *substantia*.

Here are the nine synonyms all meaning nature—in English: *nature*, *essence*, *being*, *substance*; in Latin: *natura*, *essentia*, *substantia*; in Greek: *phusis* and *ousia*.

Persons having the same nature or essence, whether it be divine, human or angelic, are said to be *consubstantial*. *Con* in Latin often means "together" and so "consubstantial" means "having the same substance together".

The bent old servant may now announce the third in the line of guests, a most important personage:

GUEST NO. 3: THE IDEA OF AN ATTRIBUTE

An attribute is that by reason of which a thing is what it is and not something else! In plain English, a ball has only one attribute—roundness. Take away roundness and it would no longer be a ball (if by ball we mean a perfect sphere: incidentally a rugby ball by this standard, is not a ball at all). Take from a sphere or ball its roundness and it may be a cube, a cone, a cylinder, a disc; but it is no longer a ball.

An attribute, therefore, is an *essential* characteristic, feature or quality of a thing, not an accidental or occasional one. It is quite true that balls have various colours—as every child knows—but their colours can be changed by dropping them in dye and yet they would be still balls. A ball may be of rubber, ivory, wool, pigskin or a thousand substances, yet it is still a ball. In other words colour, materials, size, are not a ball's essential attributes. It has but one—sphericity or roundness.

Furthermore, attributes can never change without the thing to which they belong changing. If the attributes change then the thing is changed. Take away roundness from a ball and give it squareness instead and it is no more a ball but a cube.

Attributes imply the reality of the thing or person whose they are. Attributes imply that somewhere is a reality or entity: otherwise we should be in Alice-in-Wonderland days again where the grin of the Cheshire Cat is seen but there is no cat. As a grin cannot be there without a face, no more can an attribute exist without an entity, or reality possessing it. Of nothing, nothing can be predicated. Nothing has no attributes at all (except nothingness). Nor can attributes of one substance be transferred to another without altering both.

NOTE: *Sinfulness is not an attribute of human nature.* Before introducing the next Guest, who is even now awaiting his turn, there is one further thing about this one who is taking his place with the others. As applied to human nature there is a feature called "sinfulness". Beware of calling it an attribute of human nature. It is not. Adam was created sinless, yet he was a true man. Christ was born sinless and continued so, but was a true man, made in all things like His brethren. Sin is a gangrene attacking human nature and is no more an essential part of it than is disease an essential part of the human body it conquers. "God hath made man upright" is a great principle that Solomon found (Eccles. 7. 29) though he went on to say, "but they have sought out many inventions". Preacher or personal worker can appeal to conscience, for it is always on their side; the true and best preacher and worker know instinctively this great fact and appeal to and bring out the primeval innate best in man, for the man who can trust his fellow-man in the true sense of the word brings something out of him that others never can. An appeal to what true manhood is and should do, will bring to light the best.

The innocence and faith of childhood also illustrate the nature of humanity (cp. Matt. 18. 3; Luke 18. 16).

Christ came to restore manhood to its true estate and to remove from it all the alien, parasitic growth of sin. In Rom. 2. 14, 15 Paul says, "When the Gentiles, which have not the law, do *by nature* the things contained in the law, these, having not the law, are a law unto themselves: which shew the work of the law written in their hearts, their conscience also bearing witness, and their thoughts the mean while accusing or else excusing one another."

There is in every human heart
Some not completely barren part.

GUEST NO. 4: THE IDEA OF THE ONE PERSON BUT TWO NATURES OF CHRIST

It is important to remember that when the Lord was born *He remained one Divine Person, but became possessed of two natures,* a divine and a human. The divine nature had inherent in it the ten, or more, wonderful attributes mentioned—omnipotence, omniscience, etc. The attributes of His human nature were quite different.

He was still God; unchanged and unchanging both in His person and His nature; but He took into union with His divine nature and its attributes our human nature and its attributes.

As in man the personality is in the soul not in the body, so in Christ personality is in the divine nature. Christ was a complete personality with a divine nature for eternity before the Virgin Birth.

The Son was ever a distinct person in the Godhead, and it was this divine person, not merely a divine nature, that by the Virgin Birth became incarnate. Human nature, as has been shown, is in itself impersonal. Everyone *is* a person, and *has* a nature, not *is* a nature. Christ's human nature, considered in itself, was impersonal just as man's is. Christ united with Himself and His divine nature, our human nature. He did not unite Himself with a human person. *There were thus two natures after the Incarnation—one divine and one human—but only one Person.*

This leads to the next arrival, impatient to be announced, because he is so closely allied to the last and can never bear to be separated from him. He is

GUEST NO. 5: THE IDEA OF THE COMMUNION OF ATTRIBUTES

In introducing an "attribute" as an essential quality or feature of a thing which makes it what it is, there comes a problem. Sometimes you have a thing that has two sets of contrary attributes! Whenever this occurs, when the attributes are mutally exclusive, incompatible or contradictory, there can only be one answer: however truly there may seem to be only one thing, in reality there are *two* or more. Attributes of any one thing never contradict each other.

"But," you say, "where can one find such a monstrosity?" Look in the mirror. Represented there is an immortal soul with a spiritual nature yet inhabiting a mortal body which has a physical nature. Behold the paradox! At one and the same moment the same person is both visible and invisible; mortal and immortal; physical and spiritual; material and immaterial. The former of each set of attributes belongs to the animal or physical nature, the second to the spiritual. The two sets do not mix—like red ink and blue ink mixing to produce a colour that is neither red nor blue, but purple. Nor do they cancel out to produce a mere heap of ashes. They add up—or rather they mingle in daily intercourse in a thousand normal, natural, friendly ways. This feature is called in theology the "Communion of Attributes" (the Greek term is *Koinonia Idiomaton* or fellowship of characteristics, while the Latin equivalent is *Communicatio Idiomatum*).

No one worries about this strange communion of attributes in daily life—else the following sad story would be true of all:

The centipede was happy quite
Until the frog for fun
Said, "Pray tell me which leg follows which?"
This threw him into such a pitch
He lay distracted in the ditch
Forgetting how to run!

Whether the communion of attributes is understood or not, it is none the less true and it applies to and explains the Person of Christ and the Gospel accounts of Him.

The Lord, though one Person and that a divine Person, has *two* natures, a divine and a human, each having its own distinctive set of attributes. There is no thought of mingling them as one heretic tried to do, for that would produce a hybrid thing which is neither divine nor human, for in changing the attributes the reality whose they are is changed and this cannot be. Christ cannot change any of His divine attributes or He would cease to be God. If He could have changed He never would have been God in the first place for one of the attributes of deity is unchangeability. He cannot alter or tone down or change in any way the attributes of manhood, for in that case He would no longer be a true man.

What happened can only be that He retained *both* sets of attributes, distinct and entire and unchanged. Here are some of the paradoxes in the following chart compiled from the Gospel accounts which will explain them all.

1. The Lord was said to suffer *weariness*:

He was "*wearied* with his journey" (John 4. 6)

He was "asleep on a pillow" in the boat (Mark 4. 38) and

"His sweat was as it were great drops of blood falling down to the ground." Whereupon in Gethsemane "there appeared an angel unto him from heaven, *strengthening* him (Luke 22. 43. 44) —yet God is not weary. Cp. Isa. 40. 28.

2. The Lord was also described as liable to *hunger and to thirst.*

In the temptation in the wilderness He "hungered" (Matt.

4. 2). On the Cross He exclaimed, "I thirst" (John 19. 28). Yet in Psa. 50. 12, God who is self-sufficient can neither hunger nor thirst.

3. The Lord was further portrayed as having the human attribute of *limitation of knowledge.*

   In Matt. 24. 36 He says that He does not know the hour when the Father will send Him back to this world.

   In Mark 6. 38 He does not know how many loaves and fishes He has to feed the five thousand with and asks the disciples to "go and see".

   In Mark 11. 13 He approaches a fig tree not knowing whether or not there are any fig-buds on it.

   Yet "all things are naked and opened unto the eyes of him with whom we have to do." (Heb. 4. 13; cp. Psa. 139. 1–4; Isa. 40. 28, etc.).

NOTE: In speaking of the Lord careful distinction must be made between limitation of knowledge and being subject to error. He was temporarily and voluntarily limited in knowledge (as when He was an infant) but there is no record that He ever made a mistake.

4. The Lord as man was *born in time,* though as God He is, by eternal generation of the Father, from eternity, and He inhabits it. (Cp. Psa. 2. 7; Luke 2. 7; Acts 13. 33 yet note Psa. 90. 2; Isa. 57. 15.) Mic. 5. 2 says of the Messiah born in Bethlehem that His "goings forth have been from of old, from everlasting" and Heb. 7. 3 that Christ the Son of God has "neither beginning of days, nor end of life".
5. The Lord was also *subject, as a true Man, to change,* and so we learn that after His birth "Jesus *increased* in wisdom and stature, and in favour with God and man" (Luke 2. 52). Of God we read that He changes not at all (Psa. 102. 26, 27); note that Heb. 1. 10–12 ascribes this divine attribute of unchangeability to Christ. So He is both changeable and unchangeable.
6. The Lord as man was *limited in location* being, while on earth, in never more than any one place at a given time. Yet God is omnipresent (e.g. Psa. 139. 7–12) and Christ too claims omnipresence. Thus in Matt. 18. 20 He says, "Where two or three are gathered together in my name, there am I in the midst of them", and in Matt. 28. 19, 20, "Go ye therefore, and teach all nations . . . and, lo, I am with you alway, even unto the end of the world." There is a *logion,* or reputed saying of Christ, which says the same. It runs, "Cleave the wood and ye shall find Me; lift the stone and I am there."

   So the same Person is both limited and unlimited in His location.

NOTE: Students need to distinguish between *ubiquity* and omnipresence. Ubiquity (from Latin, *ubique*, everywhere) means the faculty attributed to the devil of being in several places at once. This is true of him, but he is not omnipresent. He cannot come within the Veil as can the weakest Christian (Heb. 10. 19–22). Christ is not ubiquitous but omnipresent.

Before proceeding further, we may summarize, as follows:

1. The Lord had a true human nature as well as a true divine nature.
2. Each nature had its own set of attributes or features.
3. These attributes were completely different and often contradictory.
4. In the Person of Christ these two sets of attributes were *added*, that is, He possessed them both at one and the same time; but they were also distinct and unmingled.
5. In theology this adding or gathering together of varying characteristics in one person is called "the Communion of Attributes".

But the next Guest, also related to the foregoing and indeed already half introduced, is also showing signs of irritation at the delay at his being announced, and so the herald proclaims:

GUEST NO. 6: THE IDEA OF SUBJECT AND OBJECT OF WORSHIP

In theology the terms "Subject of Worship" is used for "the one who worships", and "Object of Worship" for the "one who is worshipped". Before the Second World War the Japanese worshipped their Emperor; thus he was to them an Object of Worship. The only Object of Worship that Christians acknowledge is God (1 Cor. 8. 4–6).

Turning to look at the Lord's earthly life it is haunted by the same paradox. *He is both a Subject and an Object of Worship.*

He is a *Subject of Worship* in all the many passages in which He is represented as praying (e.g. Luke 6. 12, when He continues all night on a mountain in prayer to God or in Luke 22. 39–46 when He prays in Gethsemane, or in Luke 23. 34, 46 when He prays prior to His arrest and during the Crucifixion).

He is an *Object of Worship* also from first to last as in John's Gospel when, in the first chapter, He is pronounced by the strict monotheist, Nathaniel, to be "the Son of God" (John 1. 49), which title Christ does not deny. Hailed in the second last chapter by Thomas as "My Lord and my God" He gently reproves him for not having believed it before (John 20. 28, 29).

How then is Christ in this dual capacity related to the Father? Surely it is wise to announce the next waiting Guest, who can help on this very point. He is

GUEST NO. 7: THE IDEA OF THE SUBORDINATION OF THE SON TO THE FATHER

This Guest is the fact that the Son is ever subordinate to the Father as the Eternal Son and—in another way—as man.

The Council of Nicea stressed three great facts: the Three Persons in the Trinity are:

1. *Co-equal* in power and glory,
2. *Co-eternal*, and
3. *Consubstantial*, i.e. having *identical* substance (Greek: *Homoousios*, from *homos* the same, and *ousia*, being) and not *similar* substance (Greek: *homoio-ousios*, from *homoios* similar or like). These are true but within the membership of the Trinity before the Virgin Birth the Son and the Spirit always stood in a distinct relation to the Father—e.g. the Father sends and commands the Son, never the Son the Father.

Coming now to the Son's relation as man, the principle of Communion of Attributes clearly explains the paradoxes.

As God the Lord is, despite the above, truly equal to the Father (cp. John 1. 1; 5. 23). As man He is subordinate, which the following passages clearly teach:

1. 1 Cor. 15. 28, where we read, "Then shall the Son also himself be subject unto him [i.e. the Father] that put all things under him, that God may be all in all."
2. 1 Cor. 3. 23; 11. 3 which says "Christ is God's" and "The head of Christ is God".
3. All passages where Christ states that the Father sent Him, or that He does the things that God has bidden Him to do, imply subordination (cp. John 5. 19, 20, 21; 14. 24; 15. 10; 17. 4; Phil. 2. 7–9; Rev. 5. 7 and many similar passages).

A LAST LOOK AT THE GUESTS

To summarize: Thus far now assembled in the Great Hall are seven important Guests—Ideas which live and move throughout the halls of theology. Still outside are yet other friendly related Ideas and one or two unfriendly ones, who are even now awaiting their turn in future chapters to be introduced as your Guests. Here are "The Seven" you already know:

1. The Idea of *Personality*—the possession of thought, feeling, will, conscience.
2. The Idea of *Nature*—essence, or being, or substance.
3. The Idea of *Attribute*—or essential characteristic, or feature, or quality.
4. The Idea of *One Person* but *two natures* in Christ.
5. The Idea of the *Communion of Attributes*—if someone has two natures the attributes of each are retained separately and unchanged.
6. The Idea of *Subject and Object of Worship*—the former being the worshipper, the latter being the one worshipped.
7. The Idea of *the Subordination of the Son to the Father*—as to His divine nature Christ being co-equal with the Father and as to His human nature subordinate.

CONCLUDING THOUGHT: THE INCARNATION AND OUR RESPONSE

I John 4. 8 says, "God is love."

A feature of true love is its readiness to identify itself with its object. It rejoices with those that rejoice and weeps with those that weep (Rom. 12. 15). It "sits where they sit". It suffers sympathetically all that its object suffers. "In all their affliction he was afflicted" (Isa. 63. 9).

The Incarnation is the supreme instance of this feature of love as manifested by God. He did not drop salvation from heaven to earth as supplies are dropped to starving islanders by parachute. In Christ He became man, identifying Himself permanently with human nature, that He might make it partaker of His divine nature (2 Pet. 1. 4). He became what man is that man might become what He is (2 Cor. 5. 21).

It is impossible rightly to assess the Incarnation apart from an understanding of God's love. Without a sense of this, mere nice theological discriminations or precise orthodoxy can approach to blasphemy. To stand in the presence of divine love, which thus reveals itself, and to remain unmoved, unconsecrated, content with a mental perception only, can but harden the heart. No person following these studies would wish this to be true in his or her case. Every student is therefore advised to spend time in meditation before God and to seek from Him what response He desires should be made. 2 Cor. 5. 14, 15, Phil. 2. 4–8, 1 John 4. 11 give three reasons why the Incarnation imposes an obligation on man.

There is no hardness like that caused by the knowledge of divine truth and divine love which is responded to by head but not by heart or will. No tutor of any spiritual standing would fail to be intensely alert for the danger signs when, with gallons of pure evangelical theology pumped upon classes, the truth does not develop a closer walk with Christ and produce a corresponding outflow to the needy in the world. Where sin is still in the life and these truths are indiscriminately poured in, there often develops a lightness towards spiritual things, a deadness and a lack of deep concern with Christ. Especially with students who have not had a great academic background does pride come in and, with it, hardness of heart. The great object in their lives becomes the attainment of external university awards rather than to know and serve the Lord better. A tutor who is a man of God will notice these signs before the session is half through and in time to call a halt for a *retreat*, for a close overhauling of life and its motives. This can take place well before the final drive for the "Finals". When the heart is right with God, the brain is divinely helped and a spiritually-minded student who works with the aid of Him "that is perfect in knowledge" should do better than a carnal one in these same examinations.

NOTES

NOTES

ADVANCE QUESTIONS ON CHAPTER FIVE: CHRIST'S RETENTION OF THE DIVINE ATTRIBUTES

1. Would it be true to say that Christ laid aside all His divine attributes when He became man? Why not?

2. Read carefully Phil. 2. 6–8 and list all the things said about Christ here. Explain the passage as carefully as you can.

3. The later verses in the same passage illustrate the truth that "The Way Up is Down". Can you find other passages that say that God has exalted Christ because of His seeking to be lowest, not highest?

4. Some people take the phrase "in the *form* of God" in the above passage (Question 2) to imply that Christ had only the *semblance* and not the *reality* of deity. Can you write down any other passages of Scripture that clearly show this could not be the case?

5. Most evangelical scholars in all ages have believed that the Angel of the Lord appearing to Jacob (in Gen. 32), to Gideon (in Judges 6), and to Samson's mother (in Judges 13) were really pre-Incarnation appearances of the Lord Jesus. If so what would be the essential difference between the bodily form in which He then appeared and that seen by His disciples on the shore of the Sea of Galilee?

6. If Christ temporarily ceased to be God at His Incarnation as some say, then

(1) He never was God anyway;
(2) His atoning Death would have no value.

Would you say these two conclusions must be correct if the previous statement were true? How could you prove your opinion from Scripture?

CHAPTER FIVE

CHRIST'S RETENTION OF DIVINE ATTRIBUTES

PART A: GATECRASHER NO. 1: THE KENOSIS THEORY

1. THE ANNOUNCEMENT OF THE INTERLOPER

Before starting this study it would be well to call forward one or two of the seven guests introduced and welcomed in the last study and solicit their services in unmasking a Gatecrasher, who even now waits in the outer hall.

A gatecrasher, of course, is someone who appears at a party who does not belong there. Uninvited, unwanted, he turns up all the same. How to deal with him politely is the problem! Some years ago a duke and duchess solved it very neatly. They had been troubled for long with these brazen-faced gentry so, when putting on a vast reception at which a repetition of their visit was expected, they prepared for it as follows. At the appointed time the proper guests arrived and, with them, these gatecrashers—dressed every whit as well as they but all minus the necessary invitation card. Many and ingenious were the explanations as to why they had come without them; sweet the smiles and gracious the gestures with which they presented their apologies. Gravely and decorously the attendants ushered them all into a gorgeous side-room which had two doors. There they were left and there they were stuck. Once the *bona fide* guests had all arrived and ceremonies were well under way, with the utmost suavity the second door was opened and the gatecrashers were ushered out into the street—where they belonged!

Now in the previous study there was a type of reception together in which seven guests were introduced and welcomed. These guests were each a *bona fide*, scriptural idea. In this study the first gatecrasher appears (more to come, sad to say, later), who is also an idea, but a false, unscriptural one; albeit he comes splendidly dressed, and his language is that of a true courtier, imitating a real Bible-idea.

To make sure of the facts before his entry into the room with two doors it is necessary first to have a hurried and private conversation with two acknowledged guests, "Attribute" and "Communion of Attributes", such sworn enemies of this gatecrasher that if the three of them were left in the same room one hour there would be murder.

In this previous conversation with these two guests assurance was gained on two points.

First, an *Attribute* is an essential characteristic of a thing by reason of which it is what it is; if the attribute changes the thing changes. To alter, take from, or add to an object's attributes is impossible without altering its character, when it no longer is what it was but becomes something quite different.

Second, *Communion of Attributes* occurs when two or more things, different things (which being different of necessity have different attributes), are brought into some sort of union. When this happens there is no mingling of their attributes (like red and blue ink uniting to produce purple ink, which is neither red nor blue), nor any cancellation but, rather, two sets of quite different attributes co-exist happily and naturally.

Now the name of this Gatecrasher No. 1—for this surely is the time to announce him—is Kenosis or the Kenotic Theory. Both names come from a Greek verb, *keno-ō*, (pronounced keno-oh,) which is used in Phil. 2. 6, 7, 8 in which the Authorized Version says that Christ, "made himself of no reputation" when He came to earth. This idea says that it should be translated, "emptied Himself" (i.e. of His divine attributes).

This verb has among its other meanings two: first, and obviously, "to empty" (its root being used in another form in our word "cenotaph" which means an empty tomb), and, secondly, "to make one become nothing", i.e. to make oneself of no reputation.

It is quite true that a Greek would read either meaning into the verb *keno-ō*, and more readily the first than the second, but Bible interpretation, like everything else in everyday life, is governed by commonsense rules of consistency. For example, there is a well-known advertisement which could be read in two ways, but no law-abiding citizen would take and act upon it in any other than one of these ways, for the other would contradict the basic principles on which he lives. Here is the advertisement: "Don't kill your wife with housework; use electricity!" Just so, when a writer like Paul says over and over again that Christ is God—always was and always will be—unchanged, unchangeable—which is flatfooted if anything is and, here, in Phil. 2. 6–8 he says something about Him which could be taken two ways, one to agree with this and the other flatly to contradict it, which should be taken? Why, the question requires no answer.

2. THE CHARACTER OF THE INTERLOPER

The Kenosis Theory is a gatecrasher born in modern times. He belongs to the younger set—a bit middle-aged now—but certainly not one of the hoary variety. It is true Apollinaris, an old heresyman (died A.D. 390), is said to have remarked that the Incarnation is self-emptying—whatever he meant by that—which might have been no more than Charles Wesley's poetic utterance,

Emptied Himself of all but love.

Otherwise no ancient writer gives a glimmer of acknowledgment to the idea, despite some scholars (always wanting innovations), saying that Paul's words in Phil. 2. 6–9 are merely a quotation from a very early Christian hymn.

By the Kenosis Theory is meant that at Incarnation the Son of God, the Second Person of the Trinity, laid aside His divine attributes and lived for a time on earth without them, purely limited as a man.

At first sight this doctrine seems to have advantages of giving theologians a true man, Christ Jesus, yet retaining full faith in Christ's deity. He was God; He then laid aside His divine attributes; "He became man"; next He ascended taking again His divine attributes. What could be better and simpler? Its advocates ask, "Why do you criticise us?" He is indeed identical with the Son of God, one in essence with the Father and equal in power and glory. In becoming incarnate He "emptied Himself" of those attributes, which essentially differentiate God from man, so that the life He lived on earth was a truly human life, but without infinity, unchangeability, omniscience and all other divine attributes. Thus He lived a life subject to the conditions and limitations of humanity as are the lives of all men. By this simple means we have a real God-Man, a straightforward meaning for Incarnation, and one that chimes in well with modern trends.

3. THE IMPEACHMENT OF THE INTERLOPER

With the aid of the principles stated by our two genuine guests this well-dressed gatecrasher can be accused on the following charges.

1. Is not such an Incarnation as this no Incarnation, but only what is called a *theophany*? This word comes from the Greek *theos*, god and *phaino*, to appear, and means as stated before an appearance of deity. There are many theophanies in the Old Testament when the Lord Jesus appeared in human or angelic form, as in the unknown Wrestler with Jacob in Gen. 32. But these were not incarnations. There was not a permanent and real union of divine and human natures. In the Kenosis Theory there is a parallel to the change in form as in the fairy story of the ogre-giant whom the cat outwitted by forcing him to change himself into a mouse, whereupon

the cat ate him up! This sounds ridiculous, but it is a true analogy. To change the attributes is to change the substance.—If Christ put off and no longer had His attributes of deity: omnipresence, infinity, unchangeability, eternity, self-existence, omnipotence, omniscience, etc., He not only ceased to be God but He never was God; for one of the attributes of God is unchangeability and another, self-existence or immortality, which includes never ceasing to exist. To say while He was on earth that He *had* been God but He was now a man, is to present to us a pagan metamorphosis or a fairy-tale as quoted above, thus as a theological fairy-tale the idea can be dismissed. To talk of the Godhead "veiled in flesh" is one thing, but "*changed* into humanity", quite another. The truth is: Christ *added* humanity to His deity; He did not *exchange* His deity for humanity.

2. There is a further criticism, viz., that if the Kenosis principle of change of natures is pressed to a logical conclusion, there is no longer a Man in the glory for, if at His Incarnation the Lord laid aside His divine nature, it is logical to assume that at His Ascension He laid aside His human nature in the same way and resumed the divine nature which He had before. It is not a simultaneous and continuous possession of the two natures but a successive one—first God, then no longer God but only man, and finally at the Ascension no longer man but only God.—Instead the Bible view is that He was before Incarnation God, while on earth God, and at Ascension God—He is not a whit less God after that than He ever was. Before Incarnation He was God but not man, and after Incarnation, on earth, He was both God and man, and at Ascension, and for eternity, both God and man. Here is a diagrammatic representation of the two doctrines:

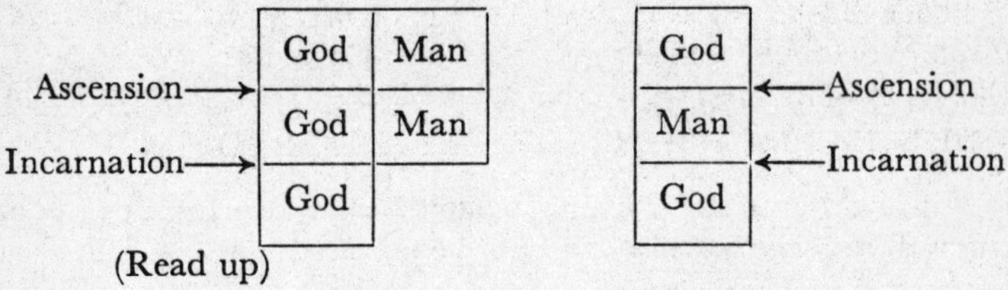

BIBLE VIEW KENOSIS THEORY

The Westminster Shorter Catechism, question 21, replies, "Who being the eternal Son of God, became man, and so was and continueth to be, God and man in two distinct natures, and one person for ever."

PART B. GUEST NO. 8: CHRIST'S RETENTION OF HIS ATTRIBUTES

1. THE NATURE OF RETENTION

Already, by contrast, the true guest is more than half introduced, whose place in this study was taken by the gatecrasher, his counterfeit, Kenosis, who has been shown the second door. This guest, the Retention of the Attributes, is beautifully illustrated by the Towel-Girdle Illustration of Retention (John 13. 1–15).

At the last Supper He laid aside His own garments, took a towel and girded Himself like a slave, and with a basin of water washed His disciples' feet. After supper He took His own garments again. Although He laid aside His ordinary garments (which can symbolize the attributes of deity), He never ceased to *possess* them; they were still His, ever within the outreach of His hands to be resumed at any moment. He did not give up the garments; He only gave up the *use* of them. *If* the towel were to represent the attributes of humanity a perfect allegory of what happened at His Ascension could be made. If Christ had wound the towel more tightly round His body and arrayed over it His outer garments again, then this symbolises His humanity being taken back with Him into heaven.

Another illustration explains the same thing in a different way. During the First World War the Prince of Wales frequently used to dress in dungarees and pay *incognito* visits to aerodromes and there tinker with the planes when many amusing and embarrassing situations would arise. On one occasion the Prince, after he had placed his hands on the propeller, was accosted by an aircraftman with the uncomplimentary challenge to take his "paws" off. "Right, old fellow," his Highness responded, "I will take my 'paws' off." But this did not stop him that very evening from resuming his court dress and full regalia and taking his place as prince at his father's side. He was as much a prince while at the hangar door as he was in the ball-room.

2. THE IMPORTANCE OF RETENTION

Retention is important for two reasons:

(1) The Retention of Attributes *is basic to the Biblical view of the Person of Christ*, for otherwise He is not and never was truly God.

(2) The Retention is also *basic to the Atonement*, for it cannot be too strongly stressed that it is the deity of Christ which makes His Atonement effective. The sacrifice of anyone less than God would never have been a satisfaction for the sins of humanity.

Rom. 6. 23 reads, "The wages of sin is death" and Heb. 9. 22 adds, "Without the shedding of blood is no remission." Now sin necessitates the death either of the offender or a divinely appointed substitute, but such a substitute must possess sufficient value in his life to cover the sins, not of one man, but of all men. Only deity could qualify for such an office.

The doctrine is so important that this repetition will serve to underline it: the value of the blood of a sheep is that of one sheep; of a man is that of one man; but of Christ, the God-Man, is that of God—it is of infinite value.

A British penny is the equivalent of one penny; a shilling is the equivalent of twelve pennies; a pound the equivalent of 240 pennies. So, if Christ at the time of His death, were only a perfect man, He could at best redeem one man; but because He is God He has paid the penalty in full for the sins of an infinite number, i.e. for all men (cp. Isa. 53. 6; John 1. 29; 1 Tim. 1. 29).

3. EXEGESIS OF PHIL. 2. 5–11

This passage is pivotal for the subject and will well repay careful translation and examination. It reads:

v. 5 "Let this mind be in you, which was also in Christ Jesus:
v. 6. "Who, being in the form (*morphē*) of God, thought it not a prize to be snatched at (*harpagmos*) to be equal with God:
v. 7 "But made himself of no reputation (*keno-ō*), and took upon himself (*heautos*) the form (*morphē*) of a slave (*doulos*), and was made in the likeness of men:
v. 8 "And being found in fashion (*schēma*) as a man, he humbled himself, and became obedient unto death, even the death of the cross.
v. 9 "Wherefore God also hath highly exalted him, and given him a name which is above every name:
v. 10 "That at the name of Jesus every knee should bow, of things in heaven, and things in earth, and things under the earth;
v. 11 "And that every tongue should confess that Jesus Christ is Lord, to the glory of God the Father."

Attention should be given first to the difference between the words "form" and "fashion". As previously shown, the word "form" in Greek is *morphē*, (pronounced morfay). It occurs in the word *metamorphosis*. *Morphē* means (1) inward substance and, (2) the outward appearance.

It is to be sharply distinguished from another Greek word, *schēma* (pronounced skaymah), here translated "fashion" (v. 8), which means the outward appearance only.

On the railway station at Slough was a stuffed animal in a glass case, called "Station Jim". Station Jim was an intelligent dog who, by the means of a collecting box strapped to his back, raised much money for the widows and orphans of Great Western Railway employees. He died in 1896. But the stuffed dog is "Station Jim" in appearance only, not in reality. The heart that beat, the arteries that pulsated, the lungs that breathed, the intelligence, the instinct —in short, the real dog—are all gone, and in their place is taxidermist's moss. There is the *schēma* but not the *morphē*.

The respective force of these two words can best be brought out by comparison with their use in other passages.

(1) **The Coming Saviour.** The first of these is Phil. 3. 21. The Authorized Version reads, "the Saviour . . . shall *change* our vile body", (R.V. "the body of our humiliation"). The Greek word for "change" is *meta-schēma-tizō*, which simply means to exchange one *schēma* for another, to transform outwardly. The passage continues, 'that it may be *fashioned like unto* his glorious body". The Revised Version gives "conformed" instead of "fashioned". The Greek is *sum-morphos*, from *sum* (or *syn*), alike or together with, and *morphē*. The redeemed body therefore will be of the same *innermost substance, as well as the same outward appearance*, as that of the Lord, (cp. 1 John 3. 2).

(2) **Transformation from within.** The second is Rom. 12. 2 where Paul says, "Be ye not conformed [Greek, *suschēmatizo*, where *sus* is *syn*] to this world: but be ye transformed [literally, 'metamorphosed', the Greek being, *meta-morpho-o*] by the renewing of your mind." His meaning is, "Do not be so like the world in outward appearance and pursuits, that you cannot be distinguished from it. Do not be like a chameleon, which takes on the colour of its surroundings, but let the inward essence [*morphē*] of what you are as a Christian show itself even in your outward appearance, and manner of life."

(3) **The Changing Glory.** The third is 2 Cor. 3. 18, "We all, with open face beholding as in a glass the glory of the Lord, are changed [*meta-morpho-omai*] into the same image from glory to glory, even as by the Spirit of the Lord." This passage teaches: (*a*) that as Christ is beheld transformation (as in Rom. 12. 2) into His very image occurs, both inwardly and even in outward appearance and manner of life. (*b*) That the vision of the Lord's glory next month should be greater than the one received today, and so on, year by year. (*c*) That the transformation of Christians' lives should similarly increase, the glory this year being far greater than that of last, hence a continual metamorphosis from one glory to another yet greater glory should ever be taking place.

4. OTHER PROOFS OF RETENTION

When Christ was upon earth He frequently gave evidence of His retention of divine attributes and prerogatives: e.g. Matt. 18. 20; Mark 2. 5–7; Luke 7. 48. These will be indicated in a later study on the deity of Christ. It is sufficient to note here that they bear directly on this matter.

PART C: THE EXALTATION OF CHRIST

1. THE WAY UP IS DOWN

In Phil. 2. 9–11 heaven's reaction is recorded to this voluntary humbling of Himself by our Lord in the exaltation to a status higher than anything He ever had even before. It is given not *in spite of*, but *because of*, His humiliation. To introduce this theme I cannot do better than quote part of one of the finest messages of the late Dr. Donald Grey Barnhouse of Philadelphia. It was given on a Sunday evening in the Big Tent of the Keswick Convention in 1953, but through the failure to receive stenographic coverage, had only the scantiest mention in "Keswick Week". The relevant part is from the writer's notes, taken verbatim at that time. The portions in italics are added by way of explanation.

"Here in this title we have the contrast between Satan's and man's way on the one hand and God's way on the other. Satan's policy is 'The Way Up is Up'; God's policy is 'The Way Up is Down'. The first is illustrated by what is said typically about Satan in Isa. 14. 1–15 and the second by what is said about the Lord Jesus in Phil. 2. 6–11.

"Until Satan's revolt there was only one will in the universe; now there are two. The biggest sin is self-will. Note the five-fold 'I will' in the Isaiah passage. *Here the prophet first addresses the great enemy of God's people, the King of Babylon and then, by the principle of dual interpretation, so frequent in Scripture, looks beyond him to the great force he typifies, Satan himself, who has inspired him. The first eleven verses speak of the earthly king and vv.* 12–15 *of his master, the devil. He is called Lucifer, Son of the Morning, (a title, like many of Satan's titles, stripped from him and given to Christ, cp.* 2 *Pet.* 1. 19; *Rev.* 2. 28; 22. 16).

"Five times in the Lucifer passage Satan says, 'I will'; 'How art thou fallen from heaven, O Lucifer, son of the morning! how art thou cut down to the ground, which didst weaken the nations! For thou hast said in thine heart, I *will* ascend into heaven, I *will* exalt my throne above the stars of God: I *will* sit also upon the mount of the congregation, in the sides of the north: I *will* ascend above the heights of the clouds; I *will* be like the most High. Yet thou shalt be brought down to hell, to the sides of the pit.'

"Sin did not begin on earth but in heaven, i.e. when Satan fell, John 8. 44; cp. Ezek. 28. 14, 15. Christ's whole teaching and action was the setting forth of the opposite principle that 'The Way Up is Down'.

"In these two passages of Scripture we have the whole philosophy of the rebellion, and of the revelation of the Son—'I will ascend' and 'I will go to the Cross'.—Here then are the rival policies of Antichrist and Christ, the world and the Spirit. Between these lies the choice that must be made in the soul of every one of you."

2. EXEGESIS OF EPH. 1. 9–10

Leaving Dr. Barnhouse's message now as it flows in other vital channels, there is another great and revealing passage in Scripture, and one which is strangely ignored. It is found in Eph. 1. 9, 10 which says that God's will is "That in the dispensation (*oiko-nomia*) of the fulness (*plērōma*) of times he might gather together (*ana-kephal-omai*) in one all things in Christ, both which are in heaven, and which are on earth; even in him."

The word translated "dispensation" comes from two Greek words, *oikos*, a house or household, and *nemo*, to manage, or distribute, or parcel out, thus the whole really means "household management". It is the origin of the English word "economics". God is regarded here as a Householder while the whole universe is God's house, and His arrangement, therefore, of its furniture, of its rules, of the personalities that shall be in authority, is simply His private "household management". He is surely entitled to make whatever changes He pleases, however drastic and sudden they may be. Indeed Paul goes on to say there is a revolutionary change that He is planning. The day and hour of it are a close secret (Matt. 24. 3), but it is fixed. It is God's D-Day.

The term Paul uses to indicate this is "in the fulness [*plērōma*] of times". *Plērōma*, like its Hebrew counterpart *melo*, means (*a*) the contents as distinguished from the container, e.g. the water as apart from the tumbler—as in the phrase, "The earth is the Lord's, and the *fulness* thereof" (Psa. 24. 1). (*b*) Further, *plērōma* tends to mean more than the actual contents. It also means their *complement*, i.e. that required to fill the glass to the brim. Thus, if a tumbler were one-third full, its *plērōma* would be the two-thirds required to top it. Therefore Paul says, "Blindness in part is happened to Israel, until the fulness (*plērōma*) of the Gentiles be come in" (Rom. 11. 25). If the final number of the saved will be ten per cent Jewish, the unfolding of the final stages of providence cannot take place till the ninety per cent Gentile complement is, through world evangelisation, brought in.

When applied in time *plērōma* has the thought of a deadline. If a passenger arrives at a railway station at 10.20 a.m. and his train is due to depart at 10.32 a.m., the "fulness of time" amounts to precisely twelve minutes, which is the period required to top up the measure to zero hour. Just so, God says, "I have appointed a zero hour for this drastic change-over in My universe administration".

Next for consideration is the word translated, "gather together into one", which is *ana-kephal-omai.* This comes from three words: first, *ana,* which here denotes "up"; then *kephale* (pronounced keffalay) which stands for "head"; and the verbal ending, *omai,* which is the Greek middle voice ending meaning "to do something for one's self". The term, therefore, has the force of gathering or summing up certain things under one head in one's own interest or to fulfil one's own purposes.

Imagine that a syndicate manufacturing automobile accessories swallows up ten small family businesses, each with its own buyer, advertising manager and sales manager and, in the interests of its economy, reorganizes all under one managing director. To express this the Greeks would use the verb, *ana-kephal-omai.*

Or consider Britain, fighting a losing battle in many theatres in the First World War, deciding to put all under one military head, Marshal Foch. To denote this again the Greeks would use the same verb, *ana-kephal-omai.*

"That," says Paul, "is exactly what the Father is to do. At present the universe is run by a lot of upstart angel changelings like the 'prince of Media' and the 'prince of Grecia', even Satan and his fallen angels (Dan. 10. 13, 20; Rev. 12. 7, 8). God in His love of souls that otherwise would be irrevocably lost puts up with it (Matt. 13. 28–30; 2 Pet. 3. 9, 15). But there is a terminus for all this; God has His zero hour in which He will bring a revolutionary change in His household management of the universe. And do you Ephesians know what He will do? He is going to put our Saviour, the Man of Galilee, Christ Jesus, in sole control of all!"

"But why," the reader may ask, "does He not do it now?" "Because," says Paul elsewhere, "the full number of His chosen ones, the total of Church members has not yet been made up." Had He set that hour for 9 a.m. on 5 September, 1850, both readers and writer of this study would have been left out. He had to wait for the Church today. Though Christ truly is Head, nevertheless there is the Body—there cannot be a Head on the Throne without also the Body on the throne. The Church, too, must sit with Him on His throne (see Rev. 3. 21, where the translation is shall "sit with me *in*—not 'on'—my Throne." The Greek word for "in" is not *epi*—on as as one would expect but *en*, meaning on the very same seat).

3. EXEGESIS OF EPH. 3. 9–11

A delightful commentary on the church's sharing Christ's rule with Him is furnished by Eph. 3. 9–11 which in the Authorized Version speaks of "the mystery" [*mustērion*, a vital secret hitherto hidden but now revealed to the initiated few] which is "that now unto the principalities and powers in heavenly places [i.e. the angelic hosts both divine and demonic] might be known [*gnōrizō*] by the church the manifold [*poikilos*, literally, variegated, hence *polupoikilos*, highly complex, manifold, "richly involved"] wisdom of God, according to the eternal purpose which he purposed in Christ Jesus our Lord."

The phrase "might be known" is a mistranslation, for the verb in this case would not be *gnōrizō*, but the related form *ginōskō*, "to know". Greek verbs ending in *izo* have a factitive or causative force, and the rendering accordingly should run, "that it might be *made known* to the principalities", etc. What this means a simple and true story will make clear.

It began at pub-closing time in the Fleet Street head office of one of Britain's most important daily newspapers. Lord ——, the proprietor, had arrived out of hours to find no one in the entire place: they had all gone out for one last drink before the night's work recommenced—no one, that is, but a typical London office boy. His Lordship stumped up and down the main hall fulminating and fuming. Then he exploded. "Here boy," he roared, "is a pretty kettle of fish! What if the king were suddenly to die—now what if he did—what would *you* do?" "Reverse the rules, sir, and roll 'em off black," instantly responded the imperturbable youth, without batting an eyelid. (Now this reply about reversing the rules happened to be exactly the thing he should have said. The brass rules between the newspaper columns have a knife edge on one side, but are thick on the other. When royalty dies they are turned upside down and the familiar thick black lines of deep mourning between the columns result.)

"See me in my office at ten o'clock tomorrow morning, boy," thundered the magnate as he turned on his heel. At ten the next day he set the lad on the second rung of a ladder that everyone knew led straight up to the highest position in the firm. It does not need much imagination to hear the private growls, complaints and other uncomplimentary remarks of the night editors and the day editors and all the hierarchy. The proprietor had gone out of his mind! What was it that in the end made known unto these principalities and powers in high-up places the multiple wisdom of the boss? It was the simple fact that the boy eventually became the most successful editor-in-chief the paper had ever known.

Satanic principalities and powers may well question the wisdom of God in appointing such puny nobodies as men to sit with Christ in His very throne when God's zero hour places Him in sole command of the universe. What will be made known in that hour to them of His manifold wisdom? *It is that Christians, united to Christ, shall make good!*

There is a further side to the Exaltation that, as the day must follow the night, so His Exaltation His Humiliation. It is in the new *glory* that He shall receive. He says of the overcomer, as already seen, "I will write upon him my new name" (Rev. 3. 12). Christ will retrieve the enjoyment of His pre-incarnation "glory" (John 17. 5), but how can He as God have a new one? How can anything be added to infinity, or how can infinite glory become greater? If God does not change, how can He have something that is new?

There is a simple answer. Travel all night across the country and, as you roar through some cities, they will flood your car with a yellow glow, others with a ruby glare and yet others with a silvery fluorescence. The high voltage electricity surging invisible for thousands of miles through the grid is unchanging—but when scaled down, in the first city it meets the resistance of sodium vapour in glass tubes it flashes into yellow light; when in the next it contacts that of neon gas, it becomes red; while if it meets mercury vapour it becomes silvery white.—God is like that.

To illustrate further, Genesis is the saga of seven men, each usually with a wife, and a counterfoil of opposite characters. Thus Abraham has his counterfoil or contrasting number in Lot, Isaac in Ishmael and Jacob in Esau. How differently the character and reaction of God show up when they come in contact with the opposite characters of these men and women! Yet it is the same God.

Never before had the invisible love of God come into immediate contact with the hate of men and the wrath of Satan, as it did in the thirty-three years of the life of the Lord Jesus. The unchangeable character of the unchanging God flashed into new, undreamed-of glories that no preceding age could ever have called forth. Yet the character of God was not changed, as the nature of the electricity from city to city was not changed. Equally Christ's Humiliation leads to an exquisite quality of glory in His Exaltation that all previous aeons of eternity could not have revealed.

SUMMARY

Christ at His Incarnation did not exchange His deity for humanity; He everlastingly added humanity to His deity.

The deity He brought with Him to earth and thereupon united with humanity was no mere pale reflection of the Godhead but its very essence.

His humiliation is rewarded by a corresponding exaltation in which glories that from eternity have been concealed are now revealed.

One day He will utterly depose Satan as ruler of the entire universe.

In all this the Jesus of History is identified inextricably with the Christ of Experience and of the Creeds. The One in His new glory is the One that was on the historical Cross, and He is in that glory simply because He was on that Cross.

NOTES

NOTES

NOTES

ADVANCE QUESTIONS ON CHAPTER SIX: THE SINLESSNESS OF CHRIST

1. The word "sin" occurs in Scripture with two quite different meanings. A careful examination of the Bible uses should serve to bring these out and explain apparent contradictions between Scriptures. Can you, by reading carefully Psa. 51. 5 and 1 John 3. 6, 8, 9, find what these are?

2. How would you reconcile the apparent discrepancy between 1 John 1. 10 and 3. 9?

3. What important task did the old High Priest of Israel have to perform which the Lord Jesus, our High Priest, did not? Why? The answer will be found in Heb. 5 and 7.

4. List as many places as you can where we are told in the Bible that Christ was without sin.

5. In the following Scriptures a number of quite different types gave testimony to Christ's innocence. Who were they and what did they say? Matt. 2. 7, 19; 27. 3, 4; Luke 4. 34; 23. 41, 47; John 19. 4, 6.

6. Read about Christ's cursing the fig-tree in Mark 11. 12–14, 20–22. How would you refute the charge against Him of (1) unreasonable demand and (2) petulant anger? (Commentaries should help you if you cannot easily find a reply.)

7. Did Christ sin when He was angry with the money-changers in the Temple and with the Pharisees? See Matt. 23. 13–36. How would you answer this?

8. Does Christ's question to the rich young ruler in Luke 18. 19 deny His own sinlessness? Give reasons.

9. Three times in the Gospels there came a divine voice from heaven. (1) In what verses are they recorded? (2) What do they imply about Christ's acceptability with the Father?

10. Can you think of any passage where Christ is specifically said (1) to offer a sacrifice for His own sins? and (2) to confess to God or man a trespass?

11. Psa. 40 is quoted as a Messianic Psalm in Heb. 10. 5–7, yet it contains a confession of sin in v. 12. Can you formulate a principle in interpreting typical Messianic prophesies that will save us from the blunder of attributing to Christ all that is found in the prophecy?

12. Why did Satan never accuse Christ of sin?

13. Write out any verses in the Epistle to the Hebrews which indi-

cate the very fact that Christ was tempted enables Him to understand and help us when we are tempted.

14. What is the difference between *trial* and *temptation*?

15. (1) Does God tempt people to sin? (Read Jas. 1.)
   (2) Who does? (Matt. 4. 1.)

16. Does God control the degree to which we are tempted? (Job 1. 8–12; 2. 3–6; 1 Cor. 10. 13.)

17. Does temptation necessarily imply sin? (Heb. 4. 15.)

18. "All things work together for good to them that love God" (Rom. 8. 28). How could this apply to temptation?

19. What two verses in Jas. 1 imply that temptation is not always a disaster?

20. Jas. 1. 13–15 seems to give a "family tree" of three generations of sin—grandparent, parent and child. What are the names of each?

21. Gen. 3. 6 and 2 Sam. 11. 2, if studied carefully, seem to push the family tree one generation back and provide a great-grandparent. What might this be?

CHAPTER SIX

THE SINLESSNESS OF CHRIST

In this study further gatecrashers are added to the company of the eight *bona fide* Guests.

It has been shown that our Lord was a Person who, at His Incarnation, combined in Himself a truly human nature with His eternally existing divine nature. Further, it has been noted that sin is accidental, not essential, to humanity, so that our Lord could be truly man without being tainted with indwelling sin. Now there is need to study what the Scripture says concerning this quality of *sinlessness* in the human nature of Christ.

This is obviously important, for God is without sin, and if Christ were not without sin, neither could He be God; yet if He were not possessed of a divine, sinless nature, the atonement would be a myth, as was noted in the previous study. In this examination are introduced:

A. THE FOUR GUESTS

GUEST NO. 9: THE IDEA OF SIN

It is logical to meet him first, for to understand what is meant by sinlessness it is essential to discover what is meant by sin.

Sin is spoken of in the Bible in a twofold way. The first Epistle of John, for instance, contains the following paradox: (1) "If we say that we have no sin, we deceive ourselves, and the truth is not in us" (1 John 1. 8) and (2) "Whosoever abideth in him sinneth not" (1 John 3. 6a) and "Whosoever is born of God doth not commit sin; for his seed remaineth in him: and he cannot sin, because he is born of God" (1 John 3. 9). A contradiction truly, but one readily explained when distinction is made between (1) Sin the STATE and (2) Sin the ACT.

1. SIN THE STATE

Sin the state is the predisposition to sin found in fallen human natures; it was referred to in an earlier chapter and is repeated here. Psa. 51. 5 says: "Behold, I was shapen in iniquity; and in sin did my mother conceive me." This is called by theologians "Original

Sin". Adam and Eve were created without it. When they fell, sin entered into their blood-stream, and thence into that of every man ever born, except Christ. Thus the first man born was a murderer.

Original Sin is that peculiar quality which sin has in our eyes, its innate affinity with *something in us that should not be there*, like a "fifth columnist" within the gates. Sin the state is like the TB bacillus in a person's blood wanting only a chill or knock for it to flare up into galloping consumption or a bovine TB joint. Such a misfortune would represent *sin the act*. Many men who have violent, uncontrollable tempers do not actually kill people but they really only need a sudden combination of particular circumstances to become murderers. While *sin the state* does not involve guilt, it makes the arrival of sin the act to be but a matter of time.

Psa. 58. 3 says that "The wicked . . . go astray as soon as they be born, speaking lies", and so also do the righteous. Dr. Donald Grey Barnhouse often told how his eighteen-month-old daughter lied before she could talk. She had a French nurse who sang to her a pretty French song to which the little girl would beat time in a charming way, gaining everybody's applause. But she also had the habit of biting her nails and this was reprimanded. One day as she was sitting up in her pram alone in the dining-room, Barnhouse suddenly entered just as she was putting her hand to her mouth to bite her nails. With the chubby little hand in mid-air she caught sight of him and instantly changed the action to one of beating time! Two thoughts chased one another across his mind. First, "She's lying!" Second, "I'm her father!"

2. SIN THE ACT

Sin the act is, as we have seen, *sin the state* coming into operation in some definite manner.

The apparent contradiction between the three passages quoted above from the Epistle of John is thus explained. In the first case the Apostle says that every man by nature has in him *sin the state.* In the second and third passages he asserts that when a man abides in Christ the counteracting force of His indwelling life keeps him, day by day, from sinning. John does not teach what is called "Sinless Perfection" (cp. 1 John 2. 1), but he states that God in Christ has made ample and sufficient provision for men *not* to sin. He has undertaken to prevent *sin the state* (which still remains in our old nature) from becoming *sin the act.*

We are now ready to introduce,

GUEST NO. 10: THE IDEA OF CHRIST'S SINLESSNESS

The word sinlessness, when applied to our Lord Jesus, implies His complete freedom, both from sin as a *state* and sin as an *act*—however infinitesimal the transgression may be as, say, the stealing of a pin.

As to *sin the state* it has been shown that the Lord was born without sin, alone of every man that has thus entered the world. The first Adam was *created* sinless; the last Adam *born* sinless. A. H. Strong well phrases it: "The portion of human nature which the Logos (i.e. The Word) took into union with Himself, was, in the very instant and by the fact of His taking it, purged from all its inherent depravity."

As to *sin the act* not occurring in Christ, Scripture gives the testimony of both God and man.

1. GOD'S TESTIMONY

Our Lord's life on earth may be divided into three parts: (1) The hidden years, thirty in all (Luke 3. 23), (2) the three years of public ministry and lastly (3) the forty days of resurrection ministry (Acts 1. 3) ending with His Ascension.

On the sinlessness of the first of these periods we have heaven's seal at the Baptism of our Lord when a voice from heaven proclaimed: "This is my beloved Son, in whom I am well pleased" (Matt. 3. 17).

Dr. G. Campbell Morgan justly remarks: "The opened heavens suggest the perfections of thirty years and declare in sacred sign and symbol that no act of His has excluded Him from the fellowship of the Perfect . . . Heaven which must for ever exclude whatsoever is imperfect could have enfolded Him without the violation of any principle of the eternal holiness." Of the first portion of the three years of public ministry again there is the Father's testimony on the snowy shoulders of Mount Hermon when, at the Transfiguration, our Lord's face, form and even His simple peasant's garments were transfigured so that the last were "shining, exceeding white as snow; so as no fuller on earth can white them" (Mark 9. 3). Again came the Voice, "This is my beloved Son; hear . . . him" (Matt. 17. 5).

On the latter portion of His public ministry the Father's seal is given a day or two before the Cross: "Then came there a voice from heaven saying, I have both glorified it, and will glorify it again" (John 12. 28).

The Resurrection, the Ascension and Pentecost are further divine seals to our Lord's sinlessness.

2. OUR LORD'S TESTIMONY

(1) Christ, though He regularly visited the temple and attended all its great sacrificial feasts, is never once represented as offering sacrifice for His own sins.

(2) He is never found confessing His own sins nor asking for forgiveness. He prayed, "Father, forgive them" (Luke 23. 34); He never prayed, "Father, forgive Me". He taught His disciples the Lord's prayer; there is no record that He ever prayed it Himself.

David's experiences often prefigured or foreshadowed Christ's, and hence those Messianic psalms that refer to them contain many expressions which Christ later took up and uttered from His own lips (e.g. Psa. 22. 1 and Matt. 27. 46). These same psalms, however, often refer to the Psalmist's *own* sins (e.g. cp. v. 12 of Psa. 40, which occurs in a Messianic Psalm, and vv. 6–8 with Heb. 10. 5–7).

Our Lord, in quoting, never repeats these confessions.

In John 8. 29 He says of His Father: "I do always those things that please him"; in John 8. 46 He asks, "Which of you convinceth me of sin?" Again in John 14. 30 He can remark, "The prince of this world . . . hath nothing in me", i.e. no grounds for an accusation.

3. THE TESTIMONY OF UNGODLY MEN AND OF THE DEVIL

If Satan, the "accuser of the brethren", had found sin in their Lord he certainly would have used the occasion to bring a case against Him, before the Father, as he did against poor Job (Job 1. 9–11; 2. 4–5).

Satan's servants, the demons, recognized His sinlessness: "I know thee who thou art; the Holy One of God" (Luke 4. 34). To theirs can be added the testimony of some not particularly innocent people: Of Judas who exclaimed: "I have betrayed the *innocent* blood" (Matt. 27. 3–4); of Pilate, who remarked: "I find no fault in him" (John 19. 4, 6); of Pilate's own wife who sent this message, "Have thou nothing to do with that just man" (Matt. 27. 19); of the malefactor who was crucified with Him and cried out: "This man *hath done nothing amiss*" (Luke 23. 41); of His executioner who exclaimed, "Certainly this was a *righteous* man" (Luke 23. 47).

4. THE TESTIMONY OF THE EARLY CHURCH

In the second proclamation of the Word on the afternoon of the day of Pentecost Peter calls Christ "The Holy One and the Just" (Acts 3.14), while a few days later the Apostles in prayer speak of

Jesus as Jehovah's "holy child" (Acts 4. 27, 30). Peter in later life never lost this conception, for he speaks of his Lord as "a lamb without blemish and without spot" (1 Pet. 1. 19) and, turning back to the Jesus of History, says that He "did no sin, neither was guile found in his mouth" (1 Pet. 2. 22).

John the beloved Apostle, sixty years after Pentecost, says: "He is pure"; "In him *is no sin*"; "He is righteous" (1 John 3. 3, 5, 7).

Ananias described Christ to Paul at his conversion as "*That Just One*" (Acts 22. 14).

Paul, applying Psa. 16. 1 to Jesus Christ, calls Him Jehovah's "*Holy One*" (Acts 13. 35). Years later he sees no reason to change this verdict for in 2 Cor. 5. 21 he writes that He "*knew no sin*".

5. THE TESTIMONY OF THE EPISTLE TO THE HEBREWS

This writing is specially important because in it the *Sinlessness of Christ* is something which is not merely implied, but made the pivot on which its whole message and proof rest. As Oscar Cullmann rightly emphasizes, this Epistle, more than any other, stresses at one and the same time both the deity and the humanity of Christ, for it sets out to present Him as High Priest. This implies Christ as the Mediator or Middleman between God and mankind and, being that, He is without fault and so acceptable and qualified to represent each.

His sinlessness is pivotal because as Mediator it is required that He must be perfect, acceptable to God as well as to man. His sinlessness is pivotal, too, because as God's High Priest He is represented as bringing mankind to perfection, and of course can only do this if He Himself is perfect.

The Greek word translated perfect is *teleios* (pronounced tell-eye-oss, from *telos*, end) means what is brought to perfection. Some scholars of the mythologizing school point out its use in the then current Mystery Religions (such as the cults of Mithras, Isis and Osiris,) as meaning not true holiness but merely what has the "cultic, sacral character of Perfection", so that it is thus a matter of ritual, not righteousness, the form not the essence and a "righteousness" that is magical rather than moral.

In the Septuagint, the Greek translation of the Old Testament, *teleio-o*, a cognate form of *teleios* is used to express Hebrew words meaning "consecration" as in Exod. 29. 9 and Lev. 8. 33, etc., where it renders a Hebrew phrase "to fill the hand", an idiom expressing consecration or dedication.

In the Epistle to the Hebrews, however, *teleios*, though it may be the identical word used both in Mystery Religions and Septuagint, points to something far more than either with their ritualistic or symbolic perfection. Heb. 2. 10 reads: "It became him, for whom are all things, and by whom are all things . . . to make the captain of their salvation *perfect through sufferings*." As sufferings include temptation this is seen as a means to perfection.

Through suffering He is said to have learned obedience: "Though he were a Son, yet learned he obedience by the things which he suffered; And being made *perfect*, he became the author of eternal salvation unto all them that obey him; Called of God (to be) an high priest" (Heb. 5. 8–10). As a High Priest He is "holy, harmless, undefiled, separate from sinners, and made higher than the heavens; who needeth not daily, as those high priests, to offer up sacrifice, first for his own sins, and then for the people's" . . . "For the law maketh men high priests which have infirmity; but the word of the oath, which was since the law, maketh the Son, who is *consecrated* [*teleio-o*] *for evermore*" (Heb. 7. 26–28).

In several passages the Lord Jesus as High Priest, being perfect Himself, makes His brothers perfect (*teleios*): e.g. Heb. 2. 10; 10. 14. Both as *Offerer and Offering He is sinless.*

(1) Of Christ as *Offerer* Heb. 4. 15 says, "We have not an high priest which cannot be touched with the feeling of our infirmities; but was in all points tempted like as we are, *yet* without sin."

(2) Of Christ as *Offering* Heb. 9. 14 reads that "Christ . . . through the eternal Spirit offered himself *without spot* to God."

Before introducing the next Guest, note that he wears humble clothing and is little thought of or discussed among men. Nevertheless he is related by ties of nature to the guests announced in this study.

NOTE: (1) The Sinless Growth of Jesus Christ

Our Lord Jesus Christ united to Himself human nature, of which *Growth* is an essential element. You are in order then to ask, "Was He sinless in His growth?"

The previous study of the word *teleios*—as mature, complete, perfect, suggests a further look at what Scripture means by development as consistent with sinlessness. In Luke 2. 52 "Jesus increased (literally struck forward, as by a series of surges) in wisdom and stature, and in favour with God and man".

Note the fourfold development of our Lord.

INtellectual	—	In wisdom
PHYsical	—	In stature
DEvotional	—	In favour with God
SOcial	—	In favour with men

A certain Young Men's Christian Association Group called themselves "The Inphydeso Club", indicating their goal as developed along these four lines. How true and balanced this is! Many seek to develop spiritually by neglecting their physical and social development, their duty to their own bodies, and their obligations to their fellow-men in the normal relationships of life, but it cannot be done. "A sound mind in a sound body" is a wonderful ideal when it is combined with a soul on fire for God. May the Lord give His church today an all-round Christian life, like our Saviour's! Neglect your body and your spiritual life will suffer.

Note that the Lord *grew* and became perfect (*teleios*) i.e. grew to maturity. This does not mean that He grew from imperfection to perfection, from sinfulness to sinlessness. The saying, "What's bred in the bone comes out in the flesh" applies here. He grew as a pure white lily that unfolds and develops, merely the unfolding of what is already latent.

NOTE: (2) The Sinlessness of Christ basic in the Creeds

The sinlessness of Christ is an essential part of every orthodox Creed. For instance in the Thirty-nine Articles, the official doctrinal basis of the Church of England, has for its fifteenth Article the following:

> "Christ in the truth of our nature was made like unto us in all things, sin only except, from which he was clearly void, both in his flesh and in his spirit. He came to be the Lamb without spot, who, by sacrifice of himself once made should take away the sins of the world, and sin, as Saint John saith, was not in Him. But all we the rest, although baptized, and born again in Christ, yet offend in many things; and if we say that we have no sin, we deceive ourselves, and the truth is not in us."

Leaving the present humble guest to make his way among his better-known relations, an inquiry is necessary into what trial and testing our Lord's sinless human nature underwent, and to help in this the next introduction is to a well-known figure:

GUEST NO. 11: THE IDEA OF TEMPTATION (See Matt. 4. 1–11)

Temptation must be distinguished from trial, which, *when used in contradistinction to temptation*, means ill which does not contain a moral element, e.g. bereavement or suffering. When Rom. 8. 28 says, "All things work together for good to them that love God", it must include both Trial and Temptation.

Temptation means testing in the forms of solicitation to evil. One's power of choice is tested—the ability to choose between what is right and what is wrong. Trial is unpleasant, temptation often pleasant, *at* the time.

Scripture clearly teaches certain truths about temptation.

1. THE TEMPTER IS THE DEVIL (Matt. 4. 1)

2. TEMPTATION IS STRICTLY CONTROLLED BY GOD

"Who," said Paul, "will not suffer you to be tempted above that ye are able" (1 Cor. 10. 13) (Job 1. 8–12; 2. 3–6).

3. TEMPTATION DOES NOT NECESSARILY IMPLY SIN

Christ "was in all points tempted like as we are, yet without sin" (Heb. 4. 15). Billy Sunday used to say, "Temptation is the devil whistling at the keyhole; sinning is opening the door and letting him in." He also said: "You can't stop the birds flying overhead but you can stop them from making nests in your hair."

4. TEMPTATION IS AMONG THE "ALL THINGS [THAT] WORK TOGETHER FOR GOOD"

No man can be the same after temptation as he was before; he is either worse or better. Satan means it should mar him; God that it should make him. Man determines which is the outcome. Jas. 1. 2, 12 says, "Brethren, count it all joy when ye fall into divers temptations . . . blessed is the man that endureth temptation." If he yields to temptation, is that no evil? It is but, if he throws himself into God's hand exactly as he is now, God will make a better thing come of the temptation than if it had never happened. He can overrule, so good comes even out of evil (see Luke 15. 22–24).

5. TEMPTATION IS A NECESSARY TEST FOR FUTURE AND HIGHER SERVICE

Every Christian is destined for a position in eternity infinitely higher than the highest earthly throne. God never sends a ship to sea without first testing it. Whether having limited capacities man is tested in a little way by little temptations suited to him, or whether, being born strong, he has to face stiffer temptations is of no consequence. The testing he undergoes now is in ratio to his ability to resist, and determines in part the position he will be allowed to hold at the Judgment Seat of Christ in His new world.

Testing is a safeguard. Some years ago a ferry, crowded to the taffrails with workmen, left New York harbour at 7.02 a.m.

When it had cast off, about 20 feet from the pier, there was one terrific bang and instantly all that remained were three planks floating on the surface. The boiler had not been tested. God is not bringing Christians to heaven to take the place which the devil once had there before his fall without first testing them. That is why Christians are often tempted to the last days of their lives—for their existence is not ending at physical death, but really only beginning.

6. THE DEVIL SERVES GOD'S PURPOSE

He is heaven's Public Inspector of Boilers No. 1. He cannot lift hand or foot without God. He may not tempt anybody that God does not want him to. He can tempt only at the precise moment God wills. He cannot tempt for one minute longer than God designs (see Rev. 2. 10):

Your days of trial then
Are all ordained by heaven;
If He have set their number ten
You ne'er shall have eleven.

The writer heard Dr. G. Campbell Morgan give a series of Bible Readings in the early twenties. He described how, as a child he gathered with other children at the door of the village smithy, to see the old master blacksmith in his leather apron tapping the metal with a tiny hammer whereat his brawny apprentice dealt it a terrific blow with his great sledge. Immediately a shower of sparks flew out, sending the children scurrying. When they reassembled they asked the master, "What are you doing with that little candy hammer of yours? You're not doing any good!" "Oh," replied he with a smile, "*I show him where to hit!*" "And," Campbell Morgan added, using these very words, "God is making the devil sweat fulfilling His purpose."

7. TEMPTATIONS ARE OF TWO SORTS

(1) The first come in the simple course of daily duty and cannot be escaped. The Lord's temptation was of this class.

(2) Other temptations, however, are induced by our own folly (cp. 1 Tim. 6. 9; Jas. 1. 14).

NOTE: The Two Families

The Unholy Family is referred to in Jas. 1. 13–15 which taken in conjunction with Gen. 3. 6 yields a family tree of four generations: Great-grandmother, Grandmother, Mother, Son. The Grandmother is *Lust*, i.e. desiring what is wrong. Our Lord's half-brother says, "Every man is tempted, when he is drawn away of his own *lust* . . . then when lust hath conceived, it bringeth forth sin: and sin, when it is finished, bringeth forth death."

The Greek nouns for "lust" and "sin" are feminine, and the verbs referring to their bearing children are only used of a woman bearing a child, not of a man. "Death" as a noun is masculine.

This verse then gives us three generations. The fourth is represented in the stories of Eve and of David. (1) In Gen. 3. 6 when "Eve *saw* the tree" she then *desired* it (this is lust, cp. "a tree to be *desired* to make one wise"), and desiring she took and ate it (this is *sin*). That day she received her sentence, which was *death*. (2) In like manner, David first *saw* Bathsheba washing; next he *desired* her; then he committed adultery and murder, which is *sin*; finally he experienced the ravages of *death* in his family and kingdom (see 2 Sam. 11. 2 ff.).

Behold, then, the Unholy Family Tree:

(1) *Seeing*, the Great-Grandmother: This is a voluntary act producing

(2) *Lust*, the Grandmother, which can be almost involuntary, giving birth to

(3) *Sin*, the Mother, which again is a voluntary act, bearing

(4) *Death*, the Son, which is involuntary.

In contrast to this we also have:

The Holy Family Tree:

(1) *Seeing*, the Great-Grandmother (e.g. "looking unto Jesus") leading to

(2) *Desiring* (what is holy and good) leading to

(3) *Doing what is right*, leading to

(4) *Life*.

Look at any collection of liquor advertisements and seventy-five per cent will present a filled glass "with beaded bubbles winking at the brim". The liquor firms know that to make a man to *see* is to force him to *desire*—to force him to desire is to drive him to *take*. Paul, on the other hand, says in Phil. 4. 8, "Whatsoever things are honest . . . just . . . pure . . . lovely . . . of good report; if there be any virtue, and if there be any praise, think on these things". The danger to Christians of carelessness in the type of books and magazines they read, and the things they see, cannot be over-emphasized. To stop desiring what is wrong may be partly out of a Christian's control, but to determine what shall be the fountainhead of desire in what is seen is a matter of free choice. To repeat, while you cannot always control your desires you can usually control the conditions that stimulate or deaden them. Read the Bible, read holy books, frequent holy places and above all keep your eyes on Christ.

Next to be announced is a guest who has a yet more intimate knowledge of the subject in hand:

GUEST NO. 12: THE IDEA OF THE TEMPTATION OF CHRIST

It must never be forgotten that this does not deal merely with a theological or a metaphysical or philosophical problem concerning the sinlessness of an isolated *Christ of the Creeds* but at the same time there is an historical problem regarding the *Jesus of History.* Once again *history affects theology: if the Jesus of History had yielded to temptation the Christ of Experience or the Creeds could not have been theologically sinless.*

There is a second link between the two. The Christ of Experience, i.e. the Jesus of your Quiet Time and who so graciously restores when fallen, is the loving, tender personality who is experienced *because He has in history met the same temptations.*

It is with renewed interest, therefore, that the cross-examination of this new guest reveals the following points:

1. THE INTIMACY OF THE ACCOUNT OF THE TEMPTATION

Matt. 4. 1–11 records the story of the Saviour's temptation by the devil. This is touching and intimate because it can only have come to the disciples through His own lips. No-one was with Him when it happened. Who but Himself could have told His disciples that it was the Father who through the Spirit arranged this temptation (Matt. 4. 1).

2. THE TIMING OF THE TEMPTATION

The principle of the mountain-top and valley-experience applies here. Directly after the mountain-top experience of the Transfiguration (Matt. 17. 1–8) came the difficult valley-experience with the demoniac boy (Matt. 17. 14–21) and immediately after the mountain-top experience at His Baptism in Jordan (Matt. 3. 13–17) came the valley-experience of the Temptation. The latter is needed to prove and test the reality of the former, while the former prepares for the latter. Temptation proves and improves faith. The rule is, when on the mountain drink in all, for you need it to be prepared for attacks immediately after. What was Christ's experience will be yours.

3. THE LONELINESS OF THE TEMPTATION

Christ had to undergo this temptation alone. After it was all over and the battle won, angels rushed to help Him (Matt. 4. 11). Why did they not come before? In a boxing match during each round the two are sparring and punching as if life depended on it. Yet the moment the signal is given the seconds dash in, crowd their hero into a corner, mop his brow and dab his eyes, rub away at him and fairly overcome him with their attentions. But they do not do it during the round! That is why the Christian has often to face temptation alone. God's seconds await in readiness to rush in the moment they are allowed. But he must undergo his try-out as his Saviour did, *alone*. But like the boxer with his seconds, the Christian is surrounded by a great cloud of witnesses (Heb. 12. 1) besides these angel-helpers (Heb. 1. 14).

4. THE REALITY OF THE TEMPTATION

Was Christ's temptation different? Did He have an easier time? Are there temptations that He did not have? Heb. 4. 15 answers all these questions when it says that He "*was in all points tempted like as we are, yet without sin*".

Was the Lord tempted as truly as men are? Some assert that as He was free from Original Sin His Temptation could not compare in reality or intensity with that to which men are subjected. But what constitutes temptation? It is solicitation to evil, and the strength of the temptation is measured by the intensity of the solicitation, from whatever source it comes, in relation to the ability to withstand it.

Solicitation to evil may be from within only, or from both within and without; but its source alone is no measure of its strength.

It is true that in man's case temptation comes both from his sinful tendencies within which, like fifth-columnists, have secret leanings towards the enemy, and from Satanic forces without. Therefore the strength of the temptation is the sum of these two, *in relation to each man's ability to withstand it*. In the case of Christ, while He did not have the fifth-columnist within, He had the full force of the Tempter without, which was as great in its proportion to His human nature as man's dual temptation is to his. With Him it was infinitely more than for mere man, for He was subjected to the sum-total of severest temptation that any man has ever been called to endure.

5. THE DANGER OF THE TEMPTATION

Could our Lord have sinned? This question puts us into the dilemma of having to choose between two Latin formulae: "*Posse non peccare*" and "*Non posse peccare*". *Posse* means "to be able" and *non* means "not" and *peccare* means "to sin". So *Posse non peccare* means "To be able not to sin", while *Non posse peccare* means "Not to be able to sin". Some evangelical theologians profess to hold one and some the other about Christ. Both parties would agree that certainly Christ did not sin during His Temptation. The point at issue is *not* this but rather, *could He have sinned*? This concerns the peccability (or ability to sin) of Christ. It is a dangerous subject and some serious splits in theological parties have occurred over it, therefore it is best to leave it alone. Where Scripture is not crystal clear it is wisest not to dogmatize. Cannot it be allowed to God to know some things that His creatures do not?

T. C. Hammond in his book *In Understanding Be Men* writes: "Scripture suggests that He was as capable of receiving temptation through His physical channels as was Adam. The older theologians describe our Lord's resistance to temptation by *posse non peccare* and not *non posse peccare*. Think of the consequences if a divine-human person really fell, and the problem at once presents itself as one of profound gravity."

As Bishop Moule truly observed, ultimately "*posse non peccare*" becomes "*non posse peccare*".

Despite these theoretic difficulties, we can be quite certain with the Scripture's light upon the following:

(1) Our Lord had two natures, a divine and a human.

(2) As to His *divine* nature He could not be tempted (Jas. 1. 13).

(3) Whether or not Christ as to His *human* nature could have sinned, the fact remains that He did not.

B. THE THREE GATECRASHERS

A gatecrasher can be one of two kinds, gracious or ungracious. The former dresses up to pass off as a *bona fide* guest and naturally behaves pleasantly as one would expect of a guest. The latter pushes his way in uninvited as a challenger and an accuser with designs to upset and embarrass both guests and hosts. The first is ushered politely out; the second is firmly removed. Three gatecrashers of the second order are encountered in this study and, while they are sworn foes to the guest just admitted, it would be fair to hear their cases before dismissing them. These three challengers of the sinlessness of Christ are: (1) The Charge of Unreasonable and Petulant Anger based on His Cursing the Fig Tree; (2) The further Charge of Anger based on His Scourging the Traders out of the Temple; (3) The Charge that He Himself admitted Sinfulness based on an imagined

Disclaimer before the Rich Young Ruler. Each will be interrogated in turn. Gatecrasher No. 1 interviewed in Chapter Five, the first is introduced as

GATECRASHER NO. 2: THE CHARGE OF UNREASONABLE AND PETULANT ANGER CONCERNING THE FIG TREE (see Mark 11. 12–14, 20–22)

In connection with this incident the critics accuse our Lord of two faults: (1) of unreasonableness in expecting fruit from a fig tree when "the time of figs was not yet", and (2) of giving way to petulant anger when His expectation was disappointed.

1. THE CHARGE OF UNREASONABLENESS

Dr. Christie, in *Palestine Calling*, makes the following observations on the incident. He points out that towards the end of March the leaves of the fig tree begin to appear, and in a week the foliage is complete. Either at the same time, or earlier, a small green bud appears about the size of an almond, which the peasant folk and hungry people eat. It is called *Taqsh.* It is not the fruit proper, but a forerunner of it. If there be no "*taqsh*" there will be no fruit that year. (The figs proper are called "*bakurat*" or "*dafur*" and appear fully formed about six weeks later.) Therefore the Lord's expectation of finding this fruit was not unreasonable.

2. THE CHARGE OF PETULANT ANGER

Note first, that there is no trace of this elsewhere in our Lord's life (cp. Isa. 53. 7; Matt. 26. 63; 27. 14; John 8. 48, 49; Heb. 12. 3; 1 Pet. 2. 23). Nor is there any indication in the Gospels that He was disturbed by the failure of earthly supplies (see Matt. 4. 3, 4; 16. 5–12; 17. 24–27). This incident of cursing the fig tree was an acted parable, setting forth (1) the obvious lesson of faith as taught by the "mustard seed" (Matt. 21), (2) the impending judgment of God upon Israel as a nation, and (3) His condemnation of an individually fruitless life.

NOTE: LESSONS FROM THE BARREN FIG TREE

(1) The fig tree is used by our Lord as a symbol of Israel in Luke 13. 6 (cp. Matt. 24. 32). There was outward profession but no fruit

("nothing but leaves"). What Christ by the power of God did to this fig tree, God later did to that generation of Israel. When our Lord ascended in glory from Olivet a few weeks later that same tree could be seen with its blanched arms, yet it was mercy, not anger, which made a warning. Christ's action has served as a salutary lesson in all ages to those who make a *profession* of Christianity unaccompanied by a manifest *possession* either of Himself as Saviour or of the fruit of the Spirit (Gal. 5. 22, 23; cp. John 15. 2, 4, 5, 8).

(2) There is a lesson for intending missionaries here. Men do not suddenly become fully-equipped workers. Experience of students in various missionary training colleges has shown that most, immediately after their conversion and years before they thought of entering a college, began to work for God. It might be either in a Sunday School class or in open-air witness or again in individual effort to win others for Christ. Their beginnings were often small and crude but they led to something larger and better. Their work was a bud, later to bear richer fruit. The Samaritan woman at once led others to the Saviour (John 4. 39); and Paul straightway preached Christ in the synagogues "that he is the Son of God" (Acts 9. 20). Many complain they are called to full-time service but no door opens. Advice to such would be: (*a*) Lay hold of God's promises concerning full-time service, believe them, and praise Him daily in faith till the hour of fulfilment. (*b*) Do all you can to bring about their fulfilment. (*c*) *Begin to work for God where you are.* Make full proof of your calling by doing all that is possible in your present restricted circumstances. "As we have therefore opportunity, let us do good" (Gal. 6. 10). Such work is like the bud which leads to the fig and, if there be no bud, there probably will never be a fig. If David had not spent his leisure moments practising with a sling there would have been no victory over Goliath (1 Sam. 17. 49–50); if he had not learned to trust God when alone he was faced with a lion and a bear (1 Sam. 17. 34–37) he could not have trusted Him when in public he was faced with a giant; if he had not mastered the art of harp-playing in his spare time he would not have had the post of court musician, which was one of the factors of his becoming king (1 Sam. 16. 14–23). Therefore do not say "There is nothing for me to do" and "No Society wants me", but start to work and do the next thing. If you follow this advice you will never be short of a task.

If you cannot cross the ocean and the heathen lands explore,
You can find the heathen nearer, you can help them at your door.
If you cannot rouse the wicked with the Judgment's dread alarms,
You can lead the little children to the Saviour's waiting arms.

GATECRASHER NO. 3: OUR LORD'S ANGER WITH THE TRADERS AND PHARISEES

The incidents referred to are recorded in Matt. 21. 12–13 and 23. 13–36, and it is objected here that Christ's anger was sinful.

Both at the beginning and the end of Christ's public ministry our Lord drove the traders violently out of the Temple (Matt. 21. 12, 13; John 2. 14–17); while in Matt. 23. 13–36 He bitterly attacked the scribes and pharisees, and in Mark 3. 5 we read that in the synagogue He "looked round about on them with anger, being grieved for the hardness of their hearts".

There is such a thing as righteous anger. It is said of God that He was angry with Moses (Deut. 1. 37), with Aaron (Deut. 9. 20), and with Solomon (1 Kings 11.9). Anger may spring from both holiness and love. It is impossible to love righteousness and not to hate unrighteousness. A mother is angry when she finds a cobra on top of her baby in its pram. This is wholly different from the anger of selfishness, or of wounded pride, or of malice.

It was love for God's honour, His law, His people, which prompted Christ's action on these occasions. Nor is righteous anger with the sinner incompatible with divine love towards him.

GATECRASHER NO. 4: OUR LORD'S APPARENT DISCLAIMER OF GOODNESS BEFORE THE RICH YOUNG RULER (LUKE 18. 18–30)

In Luke 18. 19 our Lord said to a wealthy young seeker: "Why callest thou me good? none is good, save one, that is, God." This passage is cited by some as showing that our Lord disclaimed sinlessness. The answer is that so far from doing this, rather He laid claim to deity. The Rich Young Ruler came seeking eternal life. Christ's response was two-fold. First, He showed the inquirer that, although he professed to have kept all God's commandments, he had failed to keep the spirit of them, which is love to God and man (see v. 22 and cp. Mark 12. 28–34). Secondly, He counselled the young ruler to sell all that he had and to follow Him as the One who could give treasure in heaven. The Lord's reply: "Why callest thou me good? none is good, save one, that is, God" means: "You use the word *good* too lightly. If I am really *good* I am really God," and this He consistently claimed to be.

NOTE: DEFEAT IS GOD'S HOUR FOR VICTORY

The hour of the breaking down of a man's self-confidence is one either of triumph or defeat. If it leaves him still dependent upon his own inadequate resources, it is an hour of defeat, as it was with the Rich Young Ruler. But if it forces him, like Jacob (Gen. 32. 24–30), to depend henceforth upon Him who is man's only Saviour and Hope, then it brings salvation and blessing. Christ planned a clear path for the young man. Had he but called in his failure to Him for strength he would have trodden it easily and have found eternal life here on earth and, later on, treasure in heaven. Some reader may be facing defeat and be about to resign. Yet this moment is the eve of victory because you are at the place where you give up trying to succeed yourself, and should therefore be able to cast yourself upon God. It is the hour God has been waiting for all along. He says, "Therefore will the Lord wait, that he may be gracious." (See Isa. 30. 18, with verses 7 and 15 in their context.) "Let go, and let God."

SUMMARY

The Lord was born and continued sinless throughout the thirty-three years of His earthly life. He was subjected to all the temptations to which the human race is subject, yet never sinned. The fact that He was tempted thus enables Him to help men in their temptations with understanding and sympathy, and that He remained sinless is a conditioning factor of His sacrifice for the sins of mankind being valid, and His High Priestly work acceptable.

The conception of the Sinless Christ of Experience and of the Creeds is based upon the facts of the Sinless Jesus of History. If there had been no Historical Jesus who had never sinned, there could have been no thought of His being "God manifest in the flesh". There cannot be a God manifest in the flesh and redeeming the world by His perfect sacrifice if, as the Jesus of History, He failed. The three aspects of the Lord as the central figure of History, of Experience and of Creed cannot exist without each other.

NOTES

NOTES

ADVANCE QUESTIONS ON CHAPTER SEVEN: CHRIST, THE REPRESENTATIVE MAN (1)

1. In Rom. 5. 12–21 and 1 Cor. 15. 45–47 Paul calls Christ the Last Adam and contrasts Him with the first Adam. Make a list of the things in which the two are (1) alike, (2) different.

2. In Rom. 5. 12–21 four different things are mentioned almost as if they were persons and are described as "reigning". What are they?

3. The title "Son of Man" by which the Lord described Himself (e.g. in Matt. 26. 63, 64) is almost certainly derived from Dan. 7. 13–15. The context of this passage greatly contributes to the meaning of the term. Interpret by this means the significance which you think Christ read into this term as He used it.

4. In Dan. 2, God gives to the prophet a vision of four successive world empires whose existence is terminated by a stone. (1) To whom does the stone refer? (2) What does it mean when it says that it was "cut out without hands"? and (3) that it became a mountain that filled all the earth?

CHAPTER SEVEN

CHRIST, THE REPRESENTATIVE MAN (1)

In this study we introduce as another welcome guest the Idea of Christ as the Representative Man.

When viewed in the light of the evidence supplied by this Guest, the Jesus of History, the Christ of our Experience and the Christ of the Creeds, appear as one. There is no escaping this identification, for the three will appear so bound up that they must stand or fall together.

This new friend, whom we tick off on our reception list as Guest No. 13, has a large number of brothers and sisters, and as they are a singularly united family we had no option but to present them all. The announcement of their names and the brief conversation that the occasion allows will form respectively the titles and contents of the subdivision of this and the final chapter of the present study. They are as follows:

1. The Last Adam, the Second or Heavenly Man (Guest No. 14)
2. The Son of Man (Guest No. 15)
3. The Covenanting Party (Guest No. 16)
4. The Penitent (Guest No. 17)
5. The Tempted One (Guest No. 18)
6. The Sacrifice (Guest No. 19)
7. The Ascended God-Man (Guest No. 20)

THE LAST ADAM, THE SECOND OR HEAVENLY MAN

GUEST NO. 14: THE IDEA OF REPRESENTATIVE HUMANITY

This guest is a shy one. Though there are those that have known him for long, most mature Christians have not really distinguished him from the crowd; they have never singled him out and introduced him to others. Though they may have seen him always, he melted unrecognized into the crowd of other ideas and conceptions of the Christ. Today, by laying hold of the hand of this retiring individual he is detached from the crowd and presented to the reader in his own right.

His sponsor and friend who identifies him is none other than the great Apostle Paul who, in two of his Epistles, writes particularly about him. These are 1 Corinthians and Romans; his words run as follows:

"And so it is written, The first man Adam was made a living soul; *the last Adam* was made a life-giving Spirit" (1 Cor. 15. 45).

"The first man is of the earth, earthy: *the second man is the Lord from heaven*" (1 Cor. 15. 47).

In Rom. 5. 12–21 Paul says, "By *one man* sin entered into the world, and death by sin" . . . "(If through the offence of *one* many be dead, much more the grace of God, and the gift by grace, which is by *one man*, Jesus Christ, hath abounded unto many. And not as it was by *one* that sinned, so is the gift: for the judgment was by *one* to condemnation, but the free gift is of many offences unto justification. For if by *one man*'s offence death reigned by *one*; much more they which receive abundance of grace and of the gift of righteousness shall reign in life by *one*, Jesus Christ.) Therefore, as by the offence of *one* judgment came upon all men to condemnation; even so by the righteousness of *one* the free gift came upon *all men* unto justification of life. For as by *one man*'s disobedience many were made sinners, so by the obedience of *one* shall many be made righteous . . . Where sin abounded, grace did much more abound: that as sin hath reigned unto death, even so might grace reign through righteousness unto eternal life by Jesus Christ our Lord."

The teaching of the above passages combines to give us the following results:

1. THE REPRESENTATIVENESS OF THE FIRST ADAM

In the Romans passage Paul gives a significance to Adam which can be given to no other man except Christ. Other men since Adam have lived, sinned, influenced other men and died—just as Adam did. Like Adam, those who sinned often dragged thousands more into a common ruin with themselves. But no man involved *all* men in their fall as did Adam. Adam's sin overwhelmed the whole of mankind. Without exception, of those who came after him, not one was exempt from his judgment. Every cradle means a coffin. If all mankind stemmed from him by natural generation then, through his tainted veins, sin flowed into the bloodstream of all mankind; and by this circumstance Satan and his demonic forces seized a bridgehead in this world from which to fan out and take-over all in it. The trace-element of Original Sin is in each infant's life, and he is surrounded from birth with Satanic hosts soliciting him to evil. In both epistles Paul underlines this fact. *By one man's offence sin entered and death reigned upon all.* It was not only the one affecting all but the one ruining all. Adam thus had a representativeness, a universality of influence, an absoluteness unique among all mankind.

2. THE REPRESENTATIVENESS OF CHRIST, THE LAST ADAM

Paul now goes on to say that the Lord holds a position comparable with Adam's as to His representativeness and absoluteness, and so he calls Him:

(1) The Last Adam (1 Cor. 15. 45)
(2) The Second Man (1 Cor. 15. 47) who is yet to be identified with
(3) The Lord from heaven (1 Cor. 15. 47).

NOTE: Certain traditional Bible teachers set to rights any preacher calling Christ "The second Adam" as saying that He is called only "The last Adam". Such ignore the fact that the word "Adam" while denoting a real man is simply the Hebrew term for "man", and further, that Christ is Himself called "The second man" in verse 47.

3. THE CONTRAST BETWEEN CHRIST AND ADAM

In both the Roman and the Corinthian passages Paul, having established the *analogy* between the two Adams, goes on to demonstrate the differences between them—and what a series of contrasts they present!

(1) **As to Result,** Paul the historian has outlined in Romans the story of the Four Reigns:

(*a*) The Reign of Sin (Rom. 5. 21), introducing
(*b*) The Reign of Death (Rom. 5. 14, 17), and
(*c*) The Reign of Grace (Rom. 5. 21), leading to
(*d*) The Reign of Life in the Christian whereby he also reigns with Christ (Rom. 5. 17).

The first man brought wrath, tears and woe; the Last Man brought love and joy. The one made men serfs, the Other freed the race to be princes. The first Adam was *one man*, and by this one man's disobedience to God sin and death came to usurp dominion over the entire human race—contrary to the plan and will of God. The Last Adam was *One Man*, by whose disobedience to God the reign of sin and death over mankind was overthrown and the reign of grace and righteousness unto life enthroned in their place.

The very bondslaves who were once held in so terrible a thrall are now not only under the benignant reign of life and grace but verily are made to reign themselves. Glory be to God!

(2) **As to Moral Character.** The first Adam sinned, being disobedient; the Last Adam was obedient and righteous.

(3) **As to Operation.** The consequence of the first Adam's disobedience was a matter of Law and came as an inevitable result. The result of the Last Adam's obedience came as a matter of grace (Rom. 5. 20, 21) the sovereignty of God throwing into the scale new factors which counteracted the force of Law.

(4) **As to Quality of Life.** The first Adam had merely existence. The Last Adam possessed *self-existence*, i.e. life that was not only immortal and infinite, but which carried with it the ability of its possessor to pass it on to an infinite number of beings. We read, "The last Adam (is) a life-giving Spirit": (life-giving, *zōo-poios*, pronounced zoe-oh-poyos, from *zoē*, pronounced "zoay", life, and *poieō*, to make).

(5) **As to Origin.** The first Adam was created ("was made"); the Last Adam was uncreated. The second occurrence of the phrase "was made" in 1 Cor. 15. 45 is in italics in the Authorized Version, showing that there are no words in the original Greek that are so translated, but the italicized words are supplied by the translator to make out the sense. Here the missing word, if it is to be supplied at all, should be rendered "is" to confirm to Paul's clear teaching in other places. "The last Adam *is* a life-giving Spirit."

NOTE: "Quick" is the Anglo-Saxon word for "living", and "to quicken" means therefore "to make alive" (cp. John 5. 21, Rom. 4. 17, etc.).

(6) **As to Human Will.** The first Adam's act of disobedience affects *mechanically* all mankind; the Last Adam's obedience affects *morally* all mankind. All men through the former automatically fell under death's dread sway, but all men through the latter do not automatically fall under life's sweet influence. All are redeemed and hence *potentially* saved, but they must fulfil certain moral conditions of repentance and faith, involving use of decision or will actually to be saved. Life is not an inescapable arrow, like some directed missile that searches out then chases the hostile plane high in the air till it overtakes and attaches itself to it whether it wills or not. Death following Adam's sin is just like that, but not the life which results from Christ's obedience. It is described as a "free *gift*" (Rom. 5. 16, 18), "the *gift* of righteousness" (Rom. 5. 17), and "the *gift* of grace" (Rom. 5. 15); and like all gifts, it must be voluntarily "received" (Rom. 5. 17).

(7) **As to the Personality in Question.** The first Adam was a man, a representative man granted, but nothing more. The Last

Adam was also "the Lord from heaven" whose person combined humanity with deity (1 Cor. 15. 47).

(8) **As to the Character of the Descendants.** As the first Adam, the progenitor and source from which the earthly race developed, is "earthy", so all unregenerate lives descending from him are "earthy" (1 Cor. 15. 47–50). As the Last Adam is the Progenitor and Source from which stems a heavenly race which shall inherit the kingdom of God, (said He, "Except a man be born again, he cannot see the kingdom of God",) so only the spiritually reborn descendants from the Second Adam can enter it (John 3. 3, 5). Yet at the same time it is only those who are descendants of the first Adam, who qualify as descendants of the Second Adam. No-one can be born *twice* who has not been born *once*! The new heavenly race is still like its Lord and Representative, human.

All this widespreading deliverance, then, rests upon Christ's significance, as the Great and Absolute, Representative Man.

NOTE 1: THE ORIGINAL OR HEAVENLY MAN IN NON-CHRISTIAN WRITINGS

Just as the Apostle John took hold of a term that had been in current use for over 600 years, i.e. the Logos, or Word, and gave to it a new connotation to indicate the new revelation of the Son of God as incarnate so his fellow-apostle, Paul, took hold of a series of terms which were current in Jewish and other non-Christian circles in all lands surrounding Palestine, refined and defined them, and then invested them with a new meaning. This subject, which is of prime importance for candidates in external examinations, will, like the Logos, be dealt with at some length in a future volume.

In the present one, when only a preliminary survey of the terrain is attempted, it is enough to remark without further explanation that Chaldaean, Iranian, Egyptian and other religions, including Mandaism and Manichaeism (in short those which because of their nearness to Palestine had greater contact with Jewish thought), have traces of the idea of a "divine original man", an "ideal, prototype man", a "heavenly man". It appears in quite different forms, and we are not forced to conclude that these must all have originated in a common source. The concept is also common in Gnostic systems, which usually have the notion that the original man must himself be redeemed in order to save mankind.

There was one problem, however, the Jews never quite got over—a difficulty that Paul easily solves. They frequently used to speak of Adam, the Original Man, or the Heavenly Man, in the same category as the Son of Man of Dan. 7. 13–15, who at the end of the Age comes to save Humanity (see next section). The conundrum was this: How could the Author of man's sin be at the same time the Author of man's salvation? Despite this problem many attempted to cling to the fixed idea that the Original Man of the pagan philosophers is the first man of Genesis who is equal to the Son of Man who will return at the end of the age to redeem mankind.

Some Jewish writings, like the Book of Enoch (4 Ezra) develop only the thought of the Son of Man in His end-of-the-age aspect. Some allow the Heavenly Man and the first Adam to be kept apart and not identified. In Enoch the Son of Man rises out of the sea to come in clouds, but He is not intimately incarnated into mankind as is the Original Man.

Other Jewish writers tended to get over "the Adam-problem" in one of two ways:

(1) By not equating the Heavenly Man with the First Adam.

(2) By not attributing the fall of man to Adam. Thus in the Slavonic Book of Enoch Eve, and not Adam, is tempted.

Now comes a question. This whole widely spread idea of one prototype of humanity, the archetype of man, the Original Man, the Heavenly Man, and the Last Adam who is also the eternal Son and Lord from heaven—was it all part of the primeval revelation made in Eden after the fall to the first Adam? Was it passed by tradition to his descendants and perpetuated in various garbled forms among their many races, preserved in a pure form alone in the tradition of the Old Testament, to be unfolded as a revealed "mystery" in the New? Perhaps so.

We can only here remark that to Paul who is "rightly dividing the word of truth" there is no Adam-problem. The first man, Adam, whose sorrowful remains for ever became incorporated in the soil of Armenia or some other Middle East domain nine centuries after his sinful act (Gen. 5. 3, 4), was *not* the Last Adam, but only a faint type of Him, just as Eve was not the Church but is merely a type of the Church. As with most types there is as much irreconcilable contrast as there is significant analogy, and Paul unceremoniously jettisons the former and retains only the latter.

The analogy is twofold:

(1) *As to His Person*—He is Representative of mankind and embodies all humanity within Himself.

(2) *As to His Work*—His saving act reaches to all mankind.

Above is but a mere introduction to this guest (having dismissed as well a gatecrasher or two), and he has taken his place at the end of the reception hall. (*See Oscar Cullmann*, Christology of the New Testament, *S.C.M. Press, 1959, pp. 166 ff.; Alan Richardson*, An Introduction to the Theology of the New Testament, *S.C.M. Press, 1961, pp. 242 ff.; C. H. Dodd*, The Interpretation of The Fourth

Gospel, *Camb. 1963, pp. 242 ff. After this mere introduction we dismiss our Guest but hope henceforth to invite him to tea alone for an extended chat.*)

NOTE 2: THE IMPERSONALITY OF CHRIST'S HUMAN NATURE

A fact mentioned in an earlier chapter may now be emphasized. When Christ, who was from eternity the second Person of the Trinity (i.e. the Son, the Word, the Logos), became incarnate, He took our human nature into everlasting union with His divine nature but He did not become or have a second or human personality. There is One Person only—that of the divine Son of God, and *two* natures, a human and divine. There are not two separate Persons.

Our Lord had human nature that found its personality only when it first came into contact with that divine nature. This is what is meant by the Greek term *an-hypo-stasia* (from Greek *a* or *an*, meaning *not*, and *hypo-stasis* a *person*) i.e. the impersonality of Christ's human *nature*. This does not mean that our Lord was not a perfect human man, with human reason and soul. It does mean that the conscience, feeling, thought and will of Christ's personality as a man only came into being and were developed when His human nature came into union with the personality of the Divine Logos.

But how could any "nature", human or divine, be thought of as impersonal? If the same principle is applied to nationality this point should become clear. Imagine what is meant by national character—and coin one or two words to denote it—e.g. "Russianicity"—as denoting the Slav temperament, the *esprit de corps* of the Russian nation, its outlook, way of doing things, manner of reacting. Similarly the atrocious word "Americanicity" could be coined to stand for the sum total of American characteristics or nature. Every child born in Russia tends to partake of the first nature; those in U.S.A. of the second. No reader will have any doubt in admitting this.

He will also readily admit that "Russianicity" and "Americanicity" (though only applying to persons) are not persons at all but quite impersonal. It is not Olga or Hazel, neither Ivan or Babe Ruth—but an abstract. In A. H. Strong's language: "In still plainer terms, the Logos did not take into union with Himself an already developed human person such as James, Peter, John, but human nature before it had become personal or was capable of receiving a name. It reached its personality only in union with His own divine nature. Therefore we see in Christ not two persons—a human person and a divine person—but one person, and that person possessed of a human nature as well as of a divine." (*Systematic Theology*, 12th ed., p. 679.)

Mason, quoted in the same place, says: "We count it no defect in our bodies that they have no personal subsistence apart from ourselves, and that, if separated from ourselves, they are nothing. They share in truly personal life because we, whose bodies they are, are persons. What happens to them, happens to us." (Ibid., p. 679.)

Strong continues, "In a similar manner the personality of the Logos (Word) furnished the organizing principle of Jesus' twofold nature (by 'organizing principle' he means what took two natures and made them part of one life or personality, organizing them into one living, indivisible whole). As He looked backward He could see Himself dwelling in eternity with God, so far as His divine nature was concerned; (read, for instance, John 5. 17–30, 17. 1–5, 18, 21, 23–25;) but as respects His humanity, He could remember that it was not eternal,—it had its beginnings in time. Yet this humanity had never had a separate personal existence, its personality had been developed only in connection with the divine nature." (Ibid., pp. 679–80.)

Charles Hodge writes, "The Logos (Word)—or the Son—was from all eternity a distinct Person in the Godhead. It was a *Divine Person*, not merely a Divine *nature*, that assumed humanity or became incarnate. Hence it follows that the human nature of Christ, separately considered, is impersonal. The Son of God did not unite Himself with a human *person* but with a human *nature*. There was a divine substance and a human substance; yet there was not a Divine Person *and* a human person, but only a Divine Person."

"Human nature, therefore, although endowed with intelligence and will, may be, and in fact is, in the person of Christ impersonal. That it is so is the plain doctrine of Scripture for the Son of God, a divine person, assumed a perfect human nature, and nevertheless, remains one Person." (C. Hodge, *Systematic Theology*, 2nd ed. p. 391.)

2. THE SON OF MAN

GUEST NO. 15: THE IDEA OF REPRESENTATIVE DELIVERER

This guest is a silent individual. Still waters, they say, run deep, and so do they here. He has a perfect understanding of the heart of the Lord, possessed by few others. Some facts will demonstrate this:

There is a title which is one of the very few that Christ applied to Himself and it is used only by Him, and never by any of His followers save one. After our Lord's death and within minutes of his own, Stephen, the Greek-speaking Jew, said, "I see the heavens opened, and the *Son of man* standing at the right hand of God" (Acts 7. 56). More than eighty times does the phrase occur in the four

Gospels, in all their principal sources and generally with a wealth of meaning and often with a certain pathos (e.g. Luke 9. 58).

Scores of times had God applied it to His servant, Ezekiel, when it merely meant "Man" (e.g. Ezek. 2. 1, etc.). The definitive sense, however, in which Christ employed the term is made clear in His answer to the High Priest, Caiaphas, who at His trial asked Him: "Tell us whether thou be the Christ, the Son of God?" With life, humanly speaking, depending on the answer, He replied: "Thou hast said" (implying "I am") . . . "Hereafter shall ye see the *Son of man* sitting on the right hand of power, and coming in the clouds of heaven" (Matt. 26. 63–64). This was at once taken as blasphemy and the assumption of divine prerogatives, with the inevitable consequence of a death sentence. This instance fixes the final sense as that implied by its occurrence in Daniel.

Daniel first has a vision in which the four winds of heaven, probably Satanic powers (cp. Rev. 7. 1, 2 where they are identified with four "angels"), strive upon the Great Sea (sea in Scripture is used symbolically of the unorganized but Satanically organizable mass of mankind—e.g. Rev. 13. 1; 16. 3; 21. 1), and four great beasts, which are four consecutive world empires, rise from the sea. These empires are the lion of the Babylonian Empire which ended 540 B.C. (Dan. 7. 4), the bear of the Persian Empire (Dan. 7. 5), which was overthrown in 332 B.C. by Alexander the Great whose Greek empire is the swift-moving leopard (v. 6) whose existence is swallowed up in turn by the fourth or "dreadful beast" of the Roman empire (Dan. 7. 7).

Though diverse from, and often hostile to one another, these empires yet constitute one satanically inspired *system* of world government that is opposed to God's government. The spirit, method and result of all four empires is one. This is shown by the fact (1) that the same kingdoms appear in Dan. 2 under the figure of a single *man* of whose body they represent successively the golden head, the silver breast, the brazen thigh and the iron legs, and (2) that the beast (Greek, *therion*, wild, savage beast) arising from the sea in Rev. 13. 1ff., which, in his one body, incorporates the characteristics of all the others. This fourth and final beast brings man's rule down to the end of time and the finish of all human government.

Daniel continues in vv. 9, 10, "I beheld till the thrones—i.e. of these successive world governments—were cast down, and the Ancient of days [the Father] did sit . . . A fiery stream issued and came forth from before him: thousand thousands ministered unto him, and ten thousand times ten thousand stood before him: the judgment was set, and the books were opened." Then follows a description of the judgment on the world dominions, which fixes the *time* of the appearance of the Son of man: "*I saw in the night visions, and, behold, one like the Son of man came with the clouds of heaven, and came to the Ancient of days, and they brought him near before him. And there was given him dominion, and glory, and a kingdom, that all people, nations, and languages, should serve him: his dominion is an everlasting dominion, which shall not pass away, and his kingdom that which shall not be destroyed*" (vv. 13, 14).

Daniel then asks the meaning. God tells him in vv. 17 and 18 that though the four beasts should rule yet finally, "the saints of the most High shall take the kingdom, and possess the kingdom for ever, even for ever and ever".

In vv. 21, 22 the war is to be with His saints and apparently to go against them, "Until the Ancient of days came, and judgment was given to the saints of the most High; and the time came that the saints possessed the kingdom."

This is repeated in v. 27: "The kingdom and dominion, and the greatness of the kingdom under the whole heaven, shall be given to the people of the saints of the most High, whose kingdom is an everlasting kingdom, and all dominions shall serve and obey him."

This is the exact message of the vision of Nebuchadnezzar concerning the image above referred to in Daniel 2. This is ended by the same Son of man who appears under the figure of a great Stone. We read that Daniel in relating and interpreting to the king his dream said: "Thou sawest till that a stone was cut out without hands, which smote the image upon his feet that were of iron and clay, and brake them to pieces. Then was the iron, the clay, the brass, the silver, and the gold, broken to pieces together, and became like the chaff of the summer threshingfloors; and the wind carried them away, that no place was found for them: and the stone that smote the image became a great mountain [symbol of a kingdom], and filled the whole earth" (Dan. 2. 34, 35).

Daniel continues: "In the days of these kings shall the God of heaven set up a kingdom, which shall never be destroyed: and the kingdom shall not be left to other people, but it shall break in pieces and consume all these kingdoms, and it shall stand for ever. Forasmuch as thou sawest that the stone was cut out of the mountain without hands, [that is Christ is divine and uncreated in His origin], and that it brake in pieces the iron, the brass, the clay, the silver, and the gold; the great God hath made known to the king what shall come to pass hereafter: and the dream is certain, and the interpretation thereof sure" (vv. 44, 45).

If we gather up the teaching of these two passages we have the following facts indirectly applied by the Lord Jesus to Himself in the use of the title "Son of man":

(1) The Son of man is distinct from the Father, yet He is
(2) Equal to Him, and is

(3) Identified with mankind by His very title, for He is called the Son of man, though He is yet at the same time divine.

(4) He represents and champions all men and gains for them deliverance, victory and dominion. Until He comes they are downtrodden by the great world empires and their blood poured out like water. On His arrival all this is changed. He overthrows and pulverizes those great imperial oppressors, and God's winds of judgment drive them away like chaff. To Him and to His saints dominion over the universe is now for ever granted. He reigns and, because of this, they reign, for ever.

He is thus rightly called by theologians "the eschatological Saviour", i.e. the Saviour who appears and saves His people in the end of time (Greek *eschatos*, last), and it is in this role that the Son of man appears in the flood of Jewish literature, especially that which is called apocalyptic literature (Greek *apo*, away from, *kalupto*, conceal with a veil, hence "apocalyptic" or tearing away the veil, i.e. from the future). No attention is paid as to *how* He came to be called "the Son of man". His Incarnation or Birth is not generally recorded in this literature, as is the case with the Original Man or the First Adam. He appears on the scene full-grown at the exact time He is needed to save His people.

Often the Son of man is identified and taken together with the Heavenly Man and the two are complementary. Further into this subject it is unnecessary to go at present. The guest, however, has at least been formally introduced and, as he is about to take his place with the other guests at the end of the reception hall, it is certainly our intention to call him back for an extended private conversation in a future volume. This man has been closely cross-questioned by scholars and many new facts have been discovered about him. A thorough mastery of these is, by the way, essential for those tackling external examinations.

The older theologians thought of the titles of "Son of God" and "Son of man" as denoting the twin titles of the deity and humanity of Christ respectively. This is now seen to be not quite the case. When Christ used the title of the Son of man He proclaimed His deity no less than when He used the other, and He attributed to Himself, moreover, a unique function as the Representative Man (who is yet God) in defeating for mankind his great enemy, Satan, and giving him back the kingdom he had lost at the Fall.

At Christ's first coming He broke Satan's *moral* hold of man by His putting away man's sin; at His second He will break Satan's *governmental* hold of him and will reign in his place, sharing His throne with the race which He has redeemed.

Two guests have been briefly interviewed in this chapter; the remaining five will be introduced in the next.

NOTES

NOTES

ADVANCE QUESTIONS ON CHAPTER EIGHT: CHRIST, THE REPRESENTATIVE MAN (2)

1. At His Baptism as described in Matt. 3. 13–15 our Lord was forbidden by John the Baptist to undergo the rite as not needing it but He replied that "Thus" (i.e. by doing so) it became them both to fulfil all righteousness. What did He mean?

2. Sometimes Christ's death on the Cross is represented under the figure of a slave-market, where a kind and rich man redeems and frees the slaves, and cares for them. Sometimes, as in Romans, it is represented as if within the realm of a law-court. We, the prisoners, are convicted and sentence of death is passed upon us, but One comes who pays the penalty in our place.

Beautiful and correct as are the passages in the first group, there are yet some very important factors which the second group emphasizes, and the former omits. What are these? In what respects is the first, taken alone, inadequate to describe all that Christ has done for us?

3. What important Messianic prophecy did our Lord apply to Himself in Luke 22. 37? What prophecy did the evangelist, Philip, also refer to Him in Acts 8. 30–35?

4. What words in the prophecy of the Suffering Servant of Isa. 53 indicate that (1) the Servant's death is substitutionary as an atonement, and (2) it is representative in that *one* dies for *many*?

5. In the book of Ruth are four characters, three of them women. Boaz, the fourth, has always been taken by Christian writers as a type of Christ, and they are undoubtedly right. Reading carefully the Hebrew legislation underlying Boaz' *role* as a redeemer as contained in Lev. 25. 25–34, 47–55, can you work out in what ways this wealthy Hebrew landowner of Bethlehem was a fitting foreshadower of the Redeemer of the world?

6. Is our position *today* higher or lower than that of the angels? See Psa. 8. 4–8; Gal. 4. 1–5; Heb. 2. 5–9.

7. Why was Christ tempted (as in Matt. 4. 1–11)? See Heb. 4. 15; 5. 2.

CHAPTER EIGHT

CHRIST, THE REPRESENTATIVE MAN (2)

3. THE COVENANTING PARTY

GUEST NO. 16: THE IDEA OF REPRESENTATIVE CONTRACTING

A COVENANT is an agreement or contract between two or more parties. Our human life is a tissue of such covenants and would be quite impossible without them: marriage, parenthood, building projects, taxation, military service, education, international relationships, employment, professional service, manufacture and vending, these and a thousand more institutions all imply a series of separate agreements between individuals or groups of individuals—who act on the understanding that if they abide by certain conditions, results, satisfactory to both parties, will ensue.

It is unthinkable that, if working agreements of this kind are essential in dealing with things of this life with people that are seen, there should be none in dealing with the far more important issues both of this life and the next with a God who cannot be seen. Since the first dawn of time man, once created, has lived and has died under a system of working agreements with God, which the Bible speaks of as "covenants". God has entered into these covenants not as a policeman or one playing a "cat-and-mouse" game with mankind, but in the same spirit that a man enters into a marriage covenant with a woman, to protect her interests and to secure to her for ever all that his love designs to give her.

Inherent in this tissue of human covenant relationships runs the principle of *representation.* For example, one nation threatens to go to war with a weaker nation, which promptly "sends an embassy" (Luke 14. 31, 32, R.S.V.), and desires and accepts conditions of peace. The whole nation does not go—only five or six *representatives* do so, and they do business on behalf of the rest. Thus it was with the Gibeonites (Josh. 9. 4 ff.). In labour disputes the whole union does not turn up at the management's door, for which the management is grateful, but only the leaders. In short, the *one* stands for the many.

With divine as with human covenants one law applies: a covenant can be rendered invalid if either party fails to fulfil his stipulated part of the contract. *Mere man-made covenants between God and man tend to fail because man always fails in his responsibilities—but the great covenant God has made with man is unshakable because God has not made it between Himself and mankind alone, but between Himself and all mankind as summed up in and represented by the Jesus of History, the God-Man, Christ Jesus.*

The covenants between God and man in the Bible may be said to number not one but seven—the Edenic, Adamic, Noahic, Abrahamic, Mosaic, Davidic and Messianic—yet again they are not seven but one. God did not discard them one after another, as rejects in a sort of trial-and-error process, but having announced before in the first of these His plan to make man in His own image, for an eternity of fellowship with Himself, He added the others by way of unfolding to all men for obedience to faith this great design. Each contains a reaffirmation of the central purpose of the original promise, with, in enlarged perspective, yet further and more powerful factors involved.

This system of covenants cannot be unfolded in the space here allowed, but two covenants may be mentioned and a feature in one of them dwelt upon. These are the Abrahamic and the Davidic—with their respective priestly and kingly backgrounds. The first has particular reference to the Jesus of History in His Humiliation and work on earth, the second to Christ in His Exaltation and future reign as King. It is interesting to note that both are mentioned in a single breath by Zacharias, the father of John the Baptist, the great prophet–herald of the Messiah (see Luke 1. 69–74).

Turning now to Gen. 15 we find the greatest moment in Abraham's life is recorded, the moment when God made the everlasting Abrahamic covenant with him. Directed by God he cut in two the various sacrifices thus forming a blood-sprinkled lane along which, according to Hebrew custom, he himself and the other contracting party should pass. (See Jer. 34. 18, 19 for reference to this rite.)

When, however, the supreme minute came for the treaty to be thus ratified God took care that His faithful servant was fast asleep! Instead of Abraham there proceeded instead as the *second* contracting party "a smoking furnace, and a burning lamp that passed between those pieces" (v. 17). Bible expositors in all ages have rightly understood this Lamp to be Christ, the Son.

All other covenants through Old Testament history had failed because they were made between God and man, and man always failed in his part, so the covenants became "weak and unprofitable". This covenant has endured because it is made not between God and man, but between God and the God-Man, Jesus Christ, and as He cannot fail, the covenant cannot fail.

God did not restore paradise to mankind *apart from* Christ, but *to* Christ, the true and Representative Man. He ensured that its benefits might be available to mankind by making it possible for all by faith to be united to Him. *Every blessing man enjoys is enjoyed conditionally on being united to Him.* God's covenant is made in the first place with Him, not man, and to man only as he is in Him. There is something about Christ that makes Him the representative Man—all humanity as a unity, an entity, a reality, a quality, a fact,—being summed up in Him. This covenant has only significance for men as they are identified with Him.

The Abrahamic, Davidic, and other covenants are consummated in the New or Messianic Covenant, inaugurated at the Last Supper by the Jesus of History, who then remarked as He took the cup, gave thanks and gave it to His disciples, "This is my blood of the new covenant" (*dia-thēkē*, dia-thay-kay) (see Matt. 26. 27, 28).

NOTE: The Greek for "covenant" is *diathēkē*, which occasionally means "testament" in Scripture, as it does in Heb. 10. 16, 17, but here as in nearly every other instance, "covenant", and it should so be rendered in the above passage.

Here the one *Man* represents all.

4. THE PENITENT ONE

GUEST NO. 17: THE IDEA OF REPRESENTATIVE REPENTANCE

Our Lord's Baptism is described in Matt. 3. 13–15, "Then cometh Jesus from Galilee to Jordan unto John, to be baptized of him. But John forbad him, saying, I have need to be baptized of thee, and comest thou to me? And Jesus answering said unto him, Suffer it to be so now: for *thus* it becometh us to fulfil all righteousness. Then he suffered him."

What is the force of Christ's word, "thus"? Dr. G. Campbell Morgan gives, I believe, the true answer when he points to the fact that baptism was an act of public repentance of sin, and a turning from it to wholehearted obedience to God.

The significance of this act of the Jesus of History is only recognized when it is remembered that He acted as man's representative. Here as his representative He repents of sins not His own, just as on the Cross He pays the penalty of sins not His own.

5. THE TEMPTED ONE

GUEST NO. 18: THE IDEA OF REPRESENTATIVE TEMPTATION

In the last chapter the temptation of the Lord was seen in relation to His sinlessness. Now consideration should be given to the temptation not merely of an individual person, or even of a champion deliverer of the human race, but as its representative.

When He was tempted all humanity was on probation. Similarly when He died, man died; when He rose, man rose; when He ascended, man ascended; so when He was tempted, and won, man was tempted, and won.

There were two great temptations in the three years' public ministry of Christ, one at the beginning (Matt. 4. 1–11) and one at the end in Gethsemane (Matt. 26. 36–45). Yet His whole life was one long temptation; He was under trial from the cradle to the Cross.

Here are three aspects of the significance of Christ's temptation:

(1) The first feature in the temptation is that of Christ as the representative Man, enduring and succeeding. At His temptation all humanity was tested. The keyword, therefore, for this aspect is *probation.*

(2) The second factor is Christ's consequent ability as High Priest to succour man when tempted, because He has been through the same. (See Heb. 2. 18; 4. 15, 16.) The keyword here is *experience.*

(3) The third factor is His complete victory over the devil who enslaves man. The keyword in this case is *conquest.*

NOTE 1: The temptation is viewed as the "binding of the strong man." Geerhardus Vos of Princeton (in *Biblical Theology*, p. 355 ff.) throws a sidelight upon the temptation by quoting the Master's words as found in Matt. 12. 28, 29, "If I cast out devils by the Spirit of God, then the kingdom of God is come unto you . . . How can one enter into a strong man's house, and spoil his goods, except he first bind the strong man? and then he will spoil his house."

Casting out demons is the spoiling of a strong man's palace. It is only possible because their master, Satan, whose chattels they are, has first been bound. When and how, Vos asks, did this take place? The binding of the strong man was, he suggests, in the meeting of the Son of God with Satan, and in this Satan met his master. There were various encounters (cp. John 14. 30). Vos's view then is that in the temptation Christ actually met and bound Satan.

Interesting as this view may be, we must never forget that it was the Cross which conquered Satan, for by removing man's sin it cut the one cord which allowed him a usurped authority over mankind, and broke the one barrier which prevented the authority and love of God from reaching down to man.

NOTE 2: The Temptation is viewed as the testing of the Messiah. Some scholars hold the inadequate view that our Lord's temptation as recorded in Matthew was peculiar to Him as Messiah. There is doubtless some truth here, *but certainly it cannot be the whole truth.* However messianically the temptations may be posed, Christ's answers are on the basis of specific manhood and apply in principle to all men and not to the Messiah alone. It was *mankind* in Christ as its representative that was tested, for it is:

> *Man* (not merely the Messiah) that shall not live by bread alone.
> *Man* (not just the Messiah) that shall not tempt God.
> *Man* (not only the Messiah) that shall not worship any but God.

Richard Glover, in his excellent *Teacher's Commentary on the Gospel of Matthew*, writes on 4. 3 ff., " 'If thou be the Son of God, command that these stones be made bread': a seemingly innocent suggestion. There was no harm in bread, no more harm, apparently, in making stones into bread than in changing water into wine. He needed bread. Why should He not make it? If Christ had yielded He would have made Himself *unlike* His brethren. I, in want, cannot work a miracle. I need a Saviour to stand by me in my need, and teach me how to endure and how to trust. The simple doing for His own comfort what the poor and needy could not do, would have cut the link that unites Him to us."

In the second temptation He refused to cast Himself from the pinnacle of the Temple, though His feet had stepped from star to star in their creation. In the third He never leaves the place of a true man as a *subject* of faith—but like every *common* man He, the true and representative Man, owns the right of God alone to his undivided worship.

Though Satan may tempt Christ on a purely Messianic basis, yet Christ replies on a purely human basis. His answer is what every man should give. Yet Christ throughout never denies His Messiahship. Indirectly He assumes it. He could easily have brought the whole transaction to an end by saying, "I am not the Son of God".

NOTE 3: The mythological view of the temptation. The mythological view, which no evangelical theologian would hold, is an embodiment in mythological shape of the idea of a personal conflict between Messiah and Satan, who is a stock piece in Jewish and heathen lore. The school of mythologizers says that there was no basis for the story of the temptation in history. It was the usual pattern of the Champion of Light meeting the Champion of Darkness. In this case a background of stage scenery was painted in colours supplied by the Old Testament. The challenge from this school needs separate treatment in another volume and hence can merely be mentioned here.

NOTE 4: The parabolic view of the temptation. Christ related the temptation to His disciples not with any intent that they should take it as a plain history but merely as a parable or allegory enabling them to realize what temptations He had to undergo. But the infatuated disciples changed fable into fact and narrated it as history. One can only reply that even when this unlikely view is taken, the fact remains that they were still temptations. Even symbols act as counters for realities, and parables point in story form to eternal truths.

6: THE IDEA OF REPRESENTATIVE SAVIOURHOOD: CHRIST'S REDEMPTIVE WORK FOR HUMANITY ON THE CROSS

GUEST NO. 19: THE IDEA OF CHRIST AS THE REPRESENTATIVE OFFERING

There are three background situations against which Christ is represented as saving man by His death. These are (1) the Slave-Market background—in which His work is described as *redemption*, (2) the Law-Court background—in which His work is said to be *justification*, and (3) the Priestly background—where His work is spoken of as *atonement*.

(1) THE SLAVE-MARKET BACKGROUND

Christ represents mankind in His work of redemption. In viewing Christ in this aspect the background picture is that of a poor slave chained to a post in the slave-market, and thence he is redeemed and then freed by a kind-hearted man who afterwards makes him his son. The presence of the Greek terms *agorazō*, (buy in the market, or *agora*); *ex-agorazō* (buy out of the market); *lutroō* (pronounced lutro-oh, loose by paying the redemption price); *lutron* (pronounced lootron, the redemption price paid); *anti-lutron* (the redemption price paid by someone in exchange for someone else); and *apo-lutrōsis* (either the redemption price itself or the result of the redemption price being paid, i.e. liberation. Whenever this word is used in the

New Testament it usually has the latter meaning. See Luke 21. 28; Rom. 8. 23; Eph. 1. 14; 4. 30).

The classic illustration of this background is found in the typical interpretation of the Book of Ruth. The framework of this touching idyll, where sunshine and shadow seem to chase each other over the fields of rustling, bearded barley, consists of two clauses of ancient Hebrew legislation: the law of Levirate marriage, rendering compulsory the widow's marriage to her late husband's next of kin (Deut. 25. 5–10; Matt. 22. 24), and the law of the Goel-Redeemer (Lev. 25. 25–34; Jer. 32. 7). Aided by these two enactments Ruth, the loyal but poverty-stricken stranger, was able to marry into the best family in the district and to become the ancestress of King David and of the Messiah. It is the latter which concerns this study.

The word, "goel", is the technical word for the next of kin who acts as redeemer in the Hebrew legislation of Lev. 25. 25–34, 47–55, (cp. Ruth 4. 4; Jer. 32. 7). He is the kinsman-redeemer. By this enactment if a Hebrew falls into slavery and is forced to sell himself, his family, his estate, all that he sold can be compulsorily redeemed by the next of kin. Today this is called the right of pre-emption or compulsory purchase.

It will be noted at once that the true "goel" has three qualifications, and that both Boaz and Christ had all of them. First, he must have the *right* to redeem. A millionaire if not next of kin could not redeem. Boaz was for the purpose of the story next of kin. (See Ruth 2. 20; 3. 2, 9, 12, 13; 4. 4, 9, 10.) *Christ became man that He might be man's kinsman and have the right to redeem him.*

Second, he must have the *power* to redeem. A brother who was penniless could do nothing. Boaz, however, was a "mighty man of wealth". He could look on this and that field on every side to the horizon and say, "Mine, all mine". Had Christ been only a perfect man He could have redeemed one imperfect man, and no more. *Christ is God and the value of the life He laid down for humanity was infinite. No angel could have redeemed man—only God could pay the price of man's sin.*

NOTE: As the purchase price is infinite so there is no sin so terrible that this price cannot save man from its penalty. Let no murderer think his sin beyond the atoning power of Christ's life-blood. If so, he thinks his life is of more value than that of the infinite God.

Third, he must have the *will* to redeem. A millionaire-brother who was a selfish skinflint might say, "I can, but I will not." Boaz was a man of good will and so is Christ. When, before the world, the Father asked the Son, "Will You become man and redeem for Me My world?", He said, "I will." The conversation between the

Father and the Son in which the tenor of these words is recorded is found in Psa. 40. 6–8 and interpreted in Heb. 10. 5–10.

There are thus two reasons why the Son must become true man by incarnation:

(1) The first is *that He might be able to die*, for as God He could not die. Hence Heb. 2. 9 says, "Jesus . . . was made a little lower than the angels *for the suffering of death.*"

(2) The second is *that He might represent all men.* It was as *man* that He died, that His death might be laid to the credit of man. Had He been only God this could not have been so.

2. THE LAW-COURT BACKGROUND

In this setting mankind appears as arraigned before the tribunal of Eternal Justice. His guilt is undeniable, his penalty unavoidable, and his sentence irrevocable. But One is found who, by His nature as truly *man*, may represent him as a *legal* substitute and who, by His nature as truly *God*, may constitute an *equivalent* substitute for him, however great his guilt, and for an infinite number of men, i.e. for all mankind. Accordingly the guilty criminal is not "acquitted" —this would imply that he has been found innocent, or that the charge against him for some good reason could not be made good— but he is *discharged* on the grounds that the penalty which he had incurred having now been paid by another, and the Law's claims having been fully met, it now has no further hold against him.

Whenever in the New Testament these words occur (as in Romans): *nomos* (law), *dikaioō* (dik-eye-o-oh, justify), *dikaio-sunē* (dik-eye-oss-oon-ay, justification), *krinō* (to judge), or such words as penalty, guilt, impute, pardon, judge, innocence and the like, they point to this legal, or forensic, background.

That Christ is man's Representative in this sense is basic to all description of His work in such a setting as, for instance, in Paul's Epistle to the Romans.

3. THE PRIESTLY BACKGROUND

In this background new factors appear. Remarkable as were the other two settings they leave out many important issues.

In the Slave-Market figure no representation is made of (1) sin as defilement, (2) sin as estrangement from a loving God and Father, (3) sin as constituting the breaking of God's law, (4) death and slavery as a result of guilt incurred by failure, rather than by mere misfortune, and (5) a previous relationship with the redeemer or representative.

The Law-Court picture is also inadequate for (1) the judge has neither any previous nor post-trial relations with the criminal, (2) there is no provision for any change in the accused's *nature* but only for his *status* as a freed man, and (3) no place is found for the element of *holiness*.

The Priestly background, on the other hand, is nearer to the truth for (1) sin here appears not merely as an *enslaving* evil (as in the first) nor as a *guilt-producing*, *penalty-incurring* evil (as in the second) but as a *causing defilement* and, hence (2) as a thing that *separates from fellowship with a holy and loving God and Father*, who longs for this cause of separation to be put away and for access and communion with Him to be evermore restored. (3) It further provides for a complete change in man's character—from death to life, from uncleanness to holiness, from hate to love.—This transformation is involved and is effected by (4) the procedure of the sacrificial ritual.—In Christian experience this change of *character*, as well as *status*, and *relation* is wrought by faith in the sacrifice of a lamb, typifying "the Lamb of God which taketh away the sin of the world" (John 1. 29). It is never "lambs" of God but one "Lamb". *The sacrificial Lamb represents not merely a family but the nation, or rather all mankind. Here again One dies for all, because One represents all*, and one sanctifies all.

NOTE: REPRESENTATION BY THE SERVANT

Turning from the scale-model of Type to the scale-drawing of Prophecy the principle of representation is underlined in the Servant song of Isa. 52. 13–53. 12. Christ applied this to Himself (Luke 22. 37 quoting Isa. 53. 12) as did the primitive church (cp. Acts 8. 30–35; also 4. 27, 30, where "child" (*pais*) should be rendered "servant"). Here the *One* dies for *all*; He represents all by Himself suffering for *all* and by this He saves *all*. The passage in Isa. 53 reads, "Surely *he* hath borne *our* griefs, and carried *our* sorrows; yet we did esteem him stricken, smitten of God, and afflicted. But *he* was wounded for *our* transgressions, *he* was bruised for *our* iniquities: the chastisement of *our* peace was upon *him*; and with *his* stripes *we* are healed. All *we* like sheep have gone astray; *we* have turned every one to his own way; and the Lord hath laid on *him* the iniquity of *us all* . . . By his righteous knowledge shall *my righteous servant* justify *many*; for *he* shall bear their iniquities."

Lastly, Heb. 2. 9 sheds a new light on representation. "We see Jesus, who was made a little lower than the angels *for the suffering of death . . . that he by the grace of God should taste death for every man.*" Here again, the *One* represents *all.*

7. THE ASCENDED GOD-MAN

GUEST NO. 20: THE IDEA OF REPRESENTATIVE ASCENSION

1. Heb. 2. 5–9 presents Christ, summing up and representing all humanity, as seated, crowned with glory and honour at the right hand of God. The passage finds in this the fulfilment of Psa. 8 (which Christ applied to Himself, cp. Psa. 8. 2 and Matt. 21. 16) and reads, "Unto the angels hath he [the Father] not put in subjection the world to come, whereof we speak. But one in a certain place [Psa. 8. 4–6] testified, saying, What is *man*, that thou art mindful of him? or the son of man, that thou visitest him? Thou madest him a little [i.e. for a little while] lower than the angels; thou crownedst him with glory and honour, and didst set him over the works of thy hands. Thou hast put all things in subjection under him . . . But now we see not yet all things put under him. But we see Jesus, who was made a little lower than the angels [during His earthly life] for the suffering of death, crowned with glory and honour." Just as He vicariously represented all at His Baptism, the Temptation and the Cross, so He represents all in His Ascension. It is a Man, a true and representative Man, that sits at God's right hand—and already in spirit Christians are seated beside Him (Eph. 2. 6).

NOTE: This passage in Hebrews brands as unscriptural the beautiful, old-fashioned child's hymn, "I'd like to be an angel, and with the angels stand." At present men are lower than they in certain things (Heb. 2. 7), just as the heir that is a child is inferior to his tutors and custodians (cp. Gal. 4. 1–3). Often a child who has inherited a vast estate has far less ready cash than the bailiff who runs it. This does not mean, however, either Christ while on earth was or men are legally positioned lower than the angels; even today the humblest Christian has a relationship with the Father that Gabriel would be smitten down for assuming, although the full enjoyment of this relationship is not man's yet.

Christ represents at the throne the interests of all redeemed humanity—pleading His blood and answering the fierce accuser—the *One* for the *many*, (cp. Rom. 8. 34; Heb. 12. 24; 1 John 2. 1, 2; Rev. 12. 10, 11).

NO. 8. THE FORERUNNER (Heb. 6. 19, 20)

By way of concluding this study on the representative character of the Jesus of History and the Christ of Experience turn to a moving passage in Heb. 6. 19, 20 touching the great Forerunner in heaven, who has gone on ahead, not merely to "prepare a place" for men (John 14. 2, 3), but to ensure that they reach it. The passage in question reads as follows, "Which hope we have as an anchor of the soul, both sure and stedfast, and which entereth into that within the veil; Whither the forerunner is for us entered, even Jesus, made an high priest for ever . . ."

The above passage combines two remarkable figures drawn from the spheres of tempest and temple, shipping and shrine, which are inextricably interwoven within the tapestry of a single picture. The best way to examine their intricate beauty is to look at them apart. Accordingly, leaving behind for the moment the background imagery of the veil and the tabernacle leading to the Holiest of all (Heb. 9. 3–8), where Christ as High Priest has for ever entered for man, examine first the navigation picture so daringly united with it.

It was the ancient custom for a vessel when a low ebb-tide, roughness of breakers as they curled and broke over the bar, or contrary winds and currents made it inexpedient to enter the haven, to lie outside the harbour mouth and there ride out the storm. The "Anchorius", however, bearing a token anchor rowed on alone before and fastened it to the quay within the inner harbour. The unhappy barque meanwhile lay wallowing hour after hour, with white-capped billows breaking over her from stem to stern, angry winds soughing through her tangled rigging, and treacherous seaward currents tugging mercilessly. Thence:

1. THE INVISIBLE LINE OF THE ANCHORIUS

All through the night watches how longingly would all eyes on board strain towards the twinkling shore-lights which appeared as symbols of love and home, peace, safety and plenty! Let wind, wave and tide conspire as they would, the ship could not drift for did not an invisible line link her with her destination? It only needed the harbourmaster's signal for instant, willing hands to grasp the capstan ashore and by main force haul her to her allotted berth.

In these closing days of time there are many aged Christians whose friends are all gone; whose bodies are wasted with disease; whose faculties are decayed; whose money has vanished; whose usefulness seems over; whose voyage is really ended, yet who are still in the world with its storms of conflict. They say in their hearts, "Shall I ever make the heavenly harbour? My loved ones have all crossed the bar, and what have I to live for? Why do I remain?" To such, Scripture replies, "We are saved by hope" (Rom. 8. 24), "Which hope we have as an anchor of the soul . . . within the veil" (Heb. 6. 19). Jesus Christ, the Forerunner and Anchorius, going before, has made the line fast at the heavenly inner harbour—that place which means for the navigator what the innermost shrine meant for the Israelite worshipper. The Christian is connected to Him, not with the lifeline of hempen hawser or twisted steel cable that rocks may fray asunder or tempests snap, but the unbreakable link of the life of Christ Himself. The "hopeful" is left outside because God's time for him to enter the inner harbour has not yet come. "The trying of your faith worketh patience" (Jas. 1. 4) and "patience experience; and experience hope. And hope maketh not ashamed" (Rom. 5. 4–5). He knows when the trial to achieve perfect hope is complete and will not go beyond it. Then anchor may be weighed on the heavenly shore.

Two things there are that Satan (and every fiend with him below), and that all the billows of poverty, sickness, loneliness and temptation around, cannot do: the one is break that lifeline which binds a man to Christ, to heaven, to all held dear within the harbour; the other is to prevent His drawing the Christian the moment that His time comes, to Himself in the inner haven of His immediate presence and to the society of loved ones who are not lost, but only gone before.

2. THE ANCHORIUS AS HIGH PRIEST

The passage combines two irreconcilable pictures. The first is that of Anchorius or Forerunner who, when a ship could not enter the harbour, rowed ashore with the ship's light-anchor, and fastened it to the quayside to prevent her drifting out to sea. The second is that of High Priest within the Holiest.

Moses' tabernacle was divided into three parts; the outer court, entered by all Israelites, the holy place within it, entered twice daily by certain priests through a veil, and the Holiest, approached only by the High Priest once yearly, by means of a second hanging, called simply "the veil" (Matt. 27. 51; cp. Heb. 9. 1–10, especially v. 3).

In the temple, however, the outer court was divided by a four-foot, six-inch stone wall into the court of the Gentiles without and that of Israel within. This "middle wall of partition", referred to in Eph. 2. 14, bore plaques (one of which survives) in Hebrew, Greek and Latin, threatening death to any Gentile who passed beyond the wall (see Acts 21. 27–31). This exposes the shock of incongruity as the passage conjures up the picture of a weather-beaten Anchorius, his tarry garments travel-stained, his locks windswept, his rough hands bearing the anchor, its rattling chain snaking out behind him, striding past the court of the Gentiles, past the middle wall with its death threats, past the court of Israel, whose worshippers, temple police and sleek, immaculately dressed priests, paralysed by divinely sent astonishment, are powerless to stop him—

past the first veil into the holy place then, twitching aside the sixty-foot second veil, to grapple his anchor within the Holiest of all! Such is the inescapable conclusion when the passage speaks of a *pro-dromos*, (from *pro*, "before" and the irregular verb, *trechō*, to run, —whence the English "hippodrome"—), the Forerunner, who going "within the veil" where only the High Priest might go, placed an "anchor" where hitherto was allowed only an ark.

Here, as always, when Scripture presents a genuine "inconsistency", it points to deep spiritual truth. First, when the Anchorius-Priest entered through the veil for man, it was at personal risk unknown to priests, whose unruffled life involved no sacrifice to them (but only to their victims). How wild the waves that curled and crashed about His frail skiff as He crossed the bar, how fierce the winds, how many the shoals and snags, how treacherous the eddies, only He knew!

Secondly the Anchorius went before to make it possible for man to follow Him within the veil. This was a truly revolutionary thought, for no Hebrew High Priest ever said to Israel as he entered the veil, "As I go now, so later shall you!"

Thirdly, as the pledge and instrument of this, there stretches, unknown in Old Testament priesthood, a permanent life-line every inch of the way, to link the Forerunner within the veil of God's presence in heaven with the believer outside on earth.

Here ends the first section of these studies together in the Person of Christ. These have belonged more to Systematic than to Biblical theology, a realm which you must now prepare to enter. The overall task of presenting the case for identifying the Jesus of History with the Christ of Experience and of the Creeds has barely begun. Some of the Guests and Gatecrashers of ideas and counter-ideas will have to be invited again for a prolonged interview and investigation—not least among these Guests are such as Messiah (Christ) and the Son of man. Other Guests—as Logos (Word) and Kurios (Lord)—have yet to be introduced. In the Fourth Volume we shall return to the realm of Systematic theology in examining the Second Coming of Christ.

SUMMARY

Here then is a recapitulation of some of the main themes touched on thus far:

1. Christ is the Second Person of the Trinity who for the redemption of mankind became the Jesus of History. *Chapter One.*

2. He did so by the Virgin Birth, a fact inextricably embedded in human history and a circumstance which welds the Jesus of History to the Christ of Experience. *Chapter Two.*

3. The historic fact of the Incarnation conditions the Atonement the Resurrection, the Ascension and the High Priestly ministry, and the Return of Christ. All these are essentially the activity of the Jesus of History, no less than those of the eternal Second Person of the Trinity. *Chapter Three.*

4. The paradoxes and anomalies of this union of the two natures, the divine and the human in Christ, as displayed in the acts, in the sayings and in the Person of the Jesus of History, are in the great Creeds, like the Nicene. Here they are resolved and integrated into a single statement, consistent alike with the Gospel accounts of the Jesus of History, with the proclamations of the Acts and Epistles, and with the experience of Christians. *Chapter Four.*

5. One modern theological mis-statement, the Kenosis Theory, concerning the union of the divine and human natures in Christ, shows when examined, that His humiliation as the Jesus of History is indispensable to His Exaltation as the Christ of Experience. *Chapter Five.*

6. The Jesus of History throughout His earthly life remained sinless. This sinlessness of the Jesus of History is common and essential to our experience of a sinless Christ and the creeds' definition of the same and links the three together. *Chapter Six.*

7. The Jesus of History, the Christ of Experience, and the Christ of the Creeds, appears as mankind's Representative. The Saviour's work of representation begun on earth is continued in heaven and is experienced by Christians in a thousand different ways each day. *Chapters Seven and Eight.*

With a simple story this volume closes.

It is of a remarkable painting of a man playing chess with the devil. The man is about to lose. The looks of triumph on the face of the Archfiend and of appalled dismay on the countenance of the player, shows for the latter, all too truly it is a case of "Checkmate"!

For years this picture hung in a public art gallery in the North of England, admired by thousands who, without exception, saw the picture and admitted the hopelessness of the man's situation. But one day a chess expert and his friend gazed at the painting. The expert remarked, "Did that man but know, he has only one move to make to checkmate the devil!"

Perhaps there is a reader of this study who knows all about Jesus Christ but does not know Him. Christ is not Jesus, i.e. "Jehovah my Salvation". Life's goal and meaning are uncertain or not worthwhile. Or there may be another, a Christian with a real experience of salvation, but hopelessly outclassed by the devil. "This is checkmate", are his words of despair . . . For both kinds there is one move, and only one, left. Take Jesus. He once met the devil: Light met darkness. Christ checkmated the devil at the Cross. He has played

His opening gambit and followed it up, move by move, and has won the game for every member of the human race. No Christian need be checkmated by the devil. Victory is Christ's. He waits to share it. There is only one move to make. It is simple, immediate, obvious, vital. Take Christ as your Saviour; and take Him as your Deliverer. This will be to you better proof than any treatise in every time of need that the Jesus of History is truly the Christ of your Experience and your Creed.

NOTES

NOTES

BIBLIOGRAPHY

No comprehensive or adequate Bibliography is given to the student at this stage. He certainly, however, would profit by reading T. C. Hammond's excellent primer, *In Understanding be Men* (Tyndale Press) and R. A. Torrey's Scripture-based, *What the Bible Teaches* (Oliphants).

A Bibliography giving coverage for Dip. Theol. and B.D. students and others will appear at the end of the Second Volume. It is premature to give such a list now, when the issues which these books examine have not yet been discussed.

INDICES

General Index

Scripture Index in Chronological Order

(*of which some explanation is given in this book*).

Greek and Hebrew Words

(*of which some explanation is given in the text*).

Greek

Hebrew